Portrayal of Southeast Asian Refugees in Recent American Children's Books

PORTRAYAL OF SOUTHEAST ASIAN REFUGEES IN RECENT AMERICAN CHILDREN'S BOOKS

Michael Levy

Studies in American Literature
Volume 35

The Edwin Mellen Press
Lewiston•Queenston•Lampeter

Library of Congress Cataloging-in-Publication Data

Levy, Michael M.
  Portrayal of Southeast Asian refugees in recent American children's books/Michael Levy.
    p. cm. -- (Studies in American literature ; v. 35)
  Includes bibliographical references and index.
  ISBN 0-7734-7753-5
    1. Children's literature, American--Asian American authors--History and criticism. 2. Children's literature, American--History and criticism. 3. Children--United States--Books and reading. 4. Asia, Southeastern--In literature. 5. Asian Americans in literature. 6. Race relations in literature. 7. Immigrants in literature. I. Title. II. Studies in American literature (Lewiston, N.Y.) ; v. 35.

PS153.A84 L48   2000
813'.540935203959--dc21

00-031041

This is volume 35 in the continuing series
Studies in American Literature
Volume 35 ISBN 0-7734-7753-5
SAL Series ISBN 0-88946-166-X

A CIP catalog record for this book is available from the British Library.

The Edwin Mellen Press
Box 450
Lewiston, New York
USA 14092-0450

The Edwin Mellen Press
Box 67
Queenston, Ontario
CANADA L0S 1L0

The Edwin Mellen Press, Ltd.
Lampeter, Ceredigion, Wales
UNITED KINGDOM SA48 8LT

Printed in the United States of America

Dedication

To Sandra Lindow, Scott McDonald, and Miriam Anne Min Joo Lim Levy,
my blended family.

Table of Contents

Foreword

I hadn't planned to write a book on the portrayal of Southeast Asians in American children's literature. This Foreword is therefore, in part, an attempt to explain how and why this book came to be written. Although I do teach multicultural children's literature and have published widely in a number of fields, I've always felt hesitant about doing serious critical work centered on the literature of cultures not my own. That such work can be done by outsiders, and done well, is obvious. Scholars and translators such as John Bierhorst, working with the traditional literature of a number of Native American tribes, and Charles Johnson, creating translations of Hmong folk literature, have produced fine work that satisfies any rational standard for accuracy, scholarship and cultural sensitivity. Too often, however, even the most well-meaning attempt to write about a culture with which the author is not totally familiar runs the risk of falling into factual inaccuracy and stereotype. To those who read and read about children's literature on a regular basis such problems are most often seen in failed attempts by members of a majority culture to create fiction about a minority group. The current controversy over Ann Rinaldi's *My Heart is On the Ground* (1998), a seriously flawed portrayal of life at the Carlisle Indian School in the late nineteenth-century, is the result of a particularly egregious example of the problem, which is often referred to as "cultural poaching" or "appropriation." Unfortunately, although the work of scholars rarely receives the kind of searchlight attention Rinaldi's novel is currently being subjected to, we also are capable of making such errors. It is my fondest hope that I've avoid such pitfalls, but the problem is a serious one and I will return to it on a number of occasions in these pages.

Because I cannot claim expert knowledge of Vietnamese, Hmong, or Cambodian culture or literature, one way in which I've attempted to avoid the problem of misrepresenting these groups is to make no pretence to examining the cultures themselves. Rather this study is centered on an examination of how those cultures, rightly or wrongly, accurately or inaccurately, are in fact portrayed in books, more specifically children's books, published in the United States or, in a few cases, in Great Britain or Australia. Some of the writers whose work I will be discussing, Huynh Quang Nhuong, Dia Cha, and Sothea Chiemruom for example, are themselves of various Southeast Asian ethnicities and it is undoubtedly safe to assume that when they write about their own cultures and their own first hand experiences, they know what they're talking about. Other writers discussed here, although not of Southeast Asian background, have spent many years working in and with various Southeast Asian communities. To add further complexity to the situation, however, we must take note that in some cases writers of Southeast Asian background are not actually writing about their own ethnic groups. For example in *The Clay Marble* (1991), Minfong Ho, who is Chinese (although born in Burma, raised in Thailand and currently living in the United States), writes about a Cambodian refugee camp in Thailand where she did relief work. In any case, although I have done my best to be accurate in my appraisal of the material under consideration, I would welcome corrections from readers.

I began this Foreword by saying that I did not originally intend to write a book on this subject, but here we are anyway. I've written it. Why? My original impulse to work with the material at hand was largely a personal one, stemming from two sources. Eau Claire, Wisconsin, where I live, and Menomonie, Wisconsin, where I teach at the University of Wisconsin-Stout, are located in the western part of this state just an hour or two east of the Twin Cities of Minneapolis and St. Paul, Minnesota. For some reason the Twin Cities and western Wisconsin have for many years been seen as prime resettlement territory for the Hmong, the courageous mountain people of northern Laos, Thailand, and Vietnam, who, very much to their own detriment, fought on the side of the United States during the 1970s. Being much less westernized than other refugees from Southeast Asia who came to this country in the wake of the Vietnamese and other wars in that region, the Hmong have had a particularly hard time acclimatizing to life in the U.S. Over the years I have had many Hmong students in my classes at UW-Stout and, although they differ from one to another as much as any other students, I have been continually impressed by their willingness to work hard and overcome what might easily be thought of as overwhelming difficulties to become successful business people, teachers, citizens, and political leaders. When I teach children's literature I make it a point to always include among my demonstration texts, the books I bring into class to share with the students, stories from as many of the cultures represented in my classroom as possible. When Hmong (and the occasional Vietnamese) students began to show up, however, this caused problems. Very few books were available. In fact, for a number of years quite literally the only Hmong children's book I could find anywhere was Blia Xiong and Cathy Spagnoli's *por quoi* tale *Nine-in-One, Grr! Grr!* (1989). This led me gradually into a search for more books, not only on Hmong-related topics, but also on topics related to other Southeast Asian ethnic groups.

The second source of my interest in this topic is more personal. In 1987 my wife and I adopted a baby from Korea. Korea, of course, is nowhere near Vietnam or Cambodia and its culture is in many ways quite different from those of Southeast Asia. What we soon discovered, however, was that, from the viewpoint of many of our neighbors, especially those who didn't know us, there was essentially no difference between a Korean baby, and a baby of Chinese, Japanese, Vietnamese, Hmong, or other East Asian ethnicity. Our daughter hasn't had to deal with a lot of prejudice over the past decade, but there have been a few incidents, some perpetrated by genuinely nasty people, others by people acting out of simple ignorance. On one occasion Miriam, like Nary, the Cambodian refugee protagonist of Margy Burns

Knight's *Who Belongs Here?*, was called a "gook" by a passing group of teenaged boys. For another example, I still wonder why, when my daughter was in fourth grade and her school suffered through several outbreaks of lice, that it was the Asian children, mostly Hmong and adopted Koreans, who seemed to receive the closest scrutiny, especially when it turned out that the locus of the infestation was actually one of my daughter's best friends, a cute little blond-haired girl of German-American ancestry.

Unlike many of the Southeast Asian Americans who currently reside in the United States, my daughter did not exactly come to this country as a refugee. But she did come here pretty much alone, quite literally with nothing but the clothes on her back, a small bag of baby essentials, and an envelope full of official documents. Miriam has no memory of Korea and is in most ways an all-American girl, but she also knows that in other ways she's different from her largely Caucasian friends and she has a deep and abiding interest in her ethnic and racial background. Although she's happy in the United States, she wants very much to return someday to the place where she was born, if only for a visit and a chance to reconnect with her roots. This is a trait which I strongly suspect that she shares with many, perhaps most of the Vietnamese, Hmong, and Cambodian refugees now living in the United States.

So, finally, I guess that I'm writing this book for my daughter, and for my students, and for everyone I know who had to leave the place they were born for a foreign land, including, of course, my own grandparents.

Preface

One of the less well-recognized changes in American demographics in the second half of the twentieth century involves the increasing numbers of Asian immigrants from countries other than China and Japan. Koreans began to emigrate to the United States in the 1950s, as a result of the Korean War, and Vietnamese, Cambodian, Hmong, and other refugees from Southeast Asia added to that stream after the U.S. became involved in the Vietnam War. Later, and especially after the fall of Saigon, that stream became a river, and significant numbers of Vietnamese, Cambodian, and Hmong immigrants began new lives in the U.S. While the literary community in general has been somewhat slow to pick up on the fictional and non-fictional possibilities inherent in this change in the immigration pattern, children's literature—picture books, chapter books, and some YA novels—have attempted, with varying degrees of success, to depict both the cultural background or history as well as the present state of these immigrants.

In *Refugees and Immigrants: The Southeast Asian Experience as Depicted in Recent American Children's Books*, Michael Levy provides a careful examination of the literature featuring Vietnamese, Cambodian, Hmong, and other immigrants from Southeast Asia. His examination is relevant in two ways. First, there has been relatively little critical work in this area, and Levy's study goes a long way towards redressing that situation. Second, and more important, Levy is a sympathetic critic; despite protestations that he is an outsider and, therefore, not fully qualified to speak critically about these people and their cultures, he does display a remarkably sensitive understanding of the cultures and the people about whom these books have been written. The key, I think, is that Levy understands folklore.

It is in the nature of folklore to fly below literary and even cultural radar most of the time. Folklore—all of those traditional things handed down in informal ways within a cultural group, even as small a group as the family—is "the way we do it here": the way we talk, the stories (including jokes) we tell, the proverbs we invoke, the shape of our houses, the meals we set out at ritual times, the table manners, the clothes we choose to wear, and many of our other verbal and social patterns and customs. Because these oral, social, and material traditions are acquired in an informal way, they are seldom held up for inspection; people tend to believe that their way is the right way. At best, most people are by and large ignorant of this attitude; at worst, as Jan Brunvand remarks in *The Study of American Folklore*, some people can be accused of ethnocentrism, "the assumption that one's own customs, manners, and mores are the `right' ones, and that all others are scaled out in degrees of `wrongness' from this center" (407).

Even more insidious than ethnocentrism is blindness to cultural difference, a lack of awareness that different cultures see the world in different ways. An author unaware of this is very likely to misrepresent the culture about which he or she is writing. In "Chapter Two: The Way it Might Have Been," Levy discusses two familiar types of folktales: the trickster tale and the Cinderella tale, both of which appear in variants all over the world. For example, there are elements of the Asian Cinderella tales that appear to be different from the Cinderella stories with which most westerners are familiar. Many of the Asian Cinderella stories, for example, have more violence in them than do their European counterparts (which themselves, are much more violent than the Disney retellings). Levy notes, however, that it is, in the end, difficult to tell just how authentically Asian most of these Cinderella tales are as many of the authors, on one hand, are American and may not have had access to reliable Asian texts and, on the other, do not fully acknowledge the sources they did draw from or explain the liberties they took with those sources. Is this a result of creative license, a result of lack of respect for the Asian folk and their traditional culture, or just ethnocentric ignorance?

As Levy cogently argues, the problems inherent in writing about another culture are not confined to books about Asians. Much the same sort of misrepresentation has occurred in children's picture books and young adult novels about Native Americans for more than a century. Levy focuses on Susan Jeffers' *Brother Eagle, Sister Sky: A Message from Chief Seattle,* a recent and particularly egregious example of disrespect for both truth and another culture's integrity. Levy acknowledges the problem of a "majority culture [trying to] create fiction about a minority group" and even points the finger at critics as well as fiction writers, hoping that he has been able to "avoid such pitfalls." What he only tacitly acknowledges, however, is that his awareness of the problem is exactly the way in which such pitfalls are avoided; and he is to be commended not only for the recognition that there can be problems when an author writes about a culture of which he or she is not a part and continuing to remind his readers of that problem, but also for his consistent care in dealing with other cultures' traditions throughout this volume.

If an author's ignorance of or lack of respect for the folklore of his or her subjects can result in badly-written or illustrated books, an author's knowledge of and respect for another group's folklore can be constructive and can contribute greatly to the overall quality of the writing or illustrations. In his discussion of Michele Maria Surat's *Angel Child, Dragon Child,* in "Chapter Six: Dealing With Racism," Levy notes that the Vietnamese sisters "wear their best Vietnamese-style clothes to [the first day of] school which, unfortunately, look like pajamas to their American classmates, who tease them unmercifully." In this case, Levy points out that Surat is using her knowledge of Vietnamese folk costume to create a device upon which to build a story about prejudice; in other words, the author's awareness of folklore is on a different level from that of much of her readership who may be brought to question their ethnocentric assumptions—in this specific incident, assumptions about the clothes people wear—because those American assumptions about appropriate dress have been juxtaposed with the assumptions of the Vietnamese family about what might be appropriate for the first day of school.

It is, ultimately, Levy's understanding of culture which makes the present volume such an excellent analysis of this specific literary scene and such a useful resource for anyone who wishes to know more about cultural truth (and how to evaluate it) in literature and about how attention to folklore and cultural world view is important in trans-cultural literature—especially, perhaps, in trans-cultural children's literature.

Dr. C. W. Sullivan
Department of English
East Carolina University

Acknowledgements

I would like to acknowledge the many people who have helped make this book better. First and foremost, thanks are due to Sandra Lindow, my wife, sometime co-author, and frontline editor for reading the manuscript and making numerous comments and corrections. The children's literature journal *The Lion and the Unicorn*, edited by Jack Zipes and and Louisa Smith, along with guest editor C.W. Sullivan III, published early versions of two chapters of this book. Professors Michelle Martin and Christine Lac accepted even earlier versions of those chapters as conference papers to be read in children's literature sections at the MMLA. Andy Duncan accepted an early version of one chapter to be read at an SFRA conference. Teng Lee, Ia Lee, and Ken Her read the manuscript, corrected several errors, and provided information on Hmong traditions. Chip Sullivan also read the manuscript and made suggestions. Andrew Martin Coombs read part of the manuscript and contributed useful suggestions. John Block, a producer at NBC News, provided me with information on NBC's coverage of the Benjamin Smith murders. Virginia Wolf, my colleague at the University of Wisconsin-Stout, has spent many hours discussing children's literature with me. Various members of the Children's Literature listserve have provided me with endless hours of fascinating discussion and information. I would like to acknowledge the author and publisher for permission to quote from "Learning American Farming" in *Voices from Southeast Asia* by John Tenhula (New York: Holmes & Meier, 1991); Copyright © 1991 by Holmes & Meier Publishers,

Inc. I would also like to thank the University of Wisconsin-Stout for awarding me a sabbatical in 1998 and the Maybelle Ranney Price endowed chair in 1999-2000, which provided me with both the time to write this study and the money to purchase the necessary materials. Finally I'd like to acknowledge the help I've received over the years from my many multicultural students with seeing the world from something other than a middle-class, white American perspective. Thanks are due to Choua Lee, Barb Miller, May Lor, Fatemeh Hall, Prema Monteiro, Barb Tuchel, Xiong Pao Lo, Feng-Chi Fu-Jokela, Yer Yang, Henry Setino, Yenoris Henriquez, Chong Yang, Ying Khong, Akiko Yamazaki, Pao Her, Song Lor, Debbie Chen, Pha Thao, Su-nui Escobar, Beeta Bastani, Jacky Her, Seok Yee Leong, Lisa Yih, Vang Xiong, Shun-Yu Wang, Chou Moua, Lisa Weso, Jane High Hawk, Vinh Tang, Ya-Ling Huang, Angie Zamora, Nuo Xiong, Jason Sherman, and many others.

Introduction

Cambodian Dancer

No one understands in America
The stories my grandmother told me
    When I was very, very young.
Nobody cares about the spirits of soil and water
Or even the Khmer Laos, sacred dances.

The king of Angkor, Preah Kit Mealea, sees me dance
Between the pain of my world and the pleasure
    Of the spiritual world.
I am white, very white. I am invisible. Now I am serene.
See me dance and hear the spirits as they call.
Feel the tranquility inside the community life we call
    Neighborhood, they call ghetto.

Now the feast of salutation to the moon.
The music and song continue. Can you hear them?
We play Chhoung and I dance and dance.

No one understands these things in my new land.
No one cares about the light,
Only the darkness.
             (Cambodian girl, age 17, quoted in Tenhula, 31).

    Southeast Asians form one of the largest and most widely misunderstood immigrant groups in recent United States history. More accurately, they constitute a number of extremely varied ethnic populations, ranging from the Vietnamese, a significant percentage of whom came to this country well-educated and from urban

1

backgrounds, to the Hmong, a resourceful, but almost entirely unwesternized agricultural society. Despite the existence of a few early picture books like Ruth Tooze's idyllic and unfortunately outdated *Our Rice Village in Cambodia* (1963), it was once extremely difficult for younger children of Southeast Asian background to find books in English which reflected their personal experience and their family history, but, beginning with Tran-Khanh-Tuyet's important picture book *The Little Weaver of Thai-Yen Village* (1977, rev. 1987), Mace Goldfarb's *Fighters, Refugees, Immigrants* (1982), and Michele Maria Surat and Mai's *Angel Child, Dragon Child* (1983), this began to change. Now, younger children of Vietnamese, Cambodian, Lao, Thai, Hmong, and Mien ethnicity can all find at least a few books based on their cultures, some of them folktales, others realistic portrayals in fiction or non-fiction.

My primary purpose in this book is to examine a selection of the picture books and beginning chapter books currently available in English which show the experiences of Southeast Asian refugees, both in their various homelands and in the United States. I will also occasionally refer to Young Adult novels and non-fiction accounts concerning Southeast Asians in order to compare them with the books available for younger children. Several important questions will be addressed. As portrayed in these books, to what extent do the wartime and immigration experiences of the various ethnic groups differ? What specific problems do children (and adults) coming to the United States from Southeast Asia face and what solutions do these books offer? How do the books under consideration deal with, or fail to deal with the difficult ideological issues behind the wars in Vietnam, Laos, and Cambodia. Finally, to what extent can and should these books be used with children from other ethnic groups to help them understand the Southeast Asian experience?

Among the Vietnamese-related books that will be examined are the Tran-Khanh-Tuyet and Surat volumes mentioned above, Rosemary Breckler's *Sweet Dried Apples* (1996), Sherry Garland's *The Lotus Seed* (1993) and her *My Father's Boat* (1998), Kim-Lan Tran's *Têt: The New Year* (1992), Mary Z. Holmes' *Dust of Life* (1992), Karen O'Connor's *Dan Thuy's New Life in America* (1992) and Lawrence

McKay, Jr.'s *Journey Home* (1998); Cambodian-related books to be considered include Sothea Chiemruom's *Dara's Cambodian New Year* (1994), Nancy Price Graff's *Where the River Runs* (1993), and Margy Burns Knight's *Who Belongs Here?* (1993); Hmong-related books include the Goldfarb volume, Dia Cha's *Dia's Story Cloth* (1996), Pegi Deitz Shea's *The Whispering Cloth* (1995), Brian and Heather Marchant's *A Boy Named Chong* (1992), and Ia Xiong's *The Gift, The Hmong New Year* (1996). Currently Sara Gogol's *A Mien Family* (1996) is the only widely available children's book that discusses the Mien or Yao, an ethnic group similar to but separate from the Hmong. Some of these books are non-fiction; others are fiction closely based on fact. Some were written by Vietnamese, Hmong, or Cambodian authors, most of whom lived through the experiences they describe. Others were written by European and Asian Americans who were involved in the events they relate, directly or indirectly, as social workers, missionaries, medical personnel, sponsors, second language teachers, or friends.

Following this brief introduction, I will, in Chapter One, Interpreting the Past, examine how the children's books under consideration depict the various homelands of the Cambodians, Vietnamese and Hmong as existing prior to the war. In some cases, as for example in Dia Cha's picture book Dia's *Story Cloth* or Huynh Quang Nhuong's beginning chapter book *The Land I Lost*, these depictions are first hand, based on the childhood memories of the author. Other descriptions come to us less directly through written down versions of oral histories, interviews, or the Hmong *pa'ndau* or storycloths. Some of these accounts are lightly fictionalized but essentially true to life. In Chapter Two, The Way It Might Have Been, I will look at the various Southeast Asian folk and fairytales that have appeared in picture book format. These are of considerable significance here since it is through such traditional stories that people often establish for themselves and others a sense of what is important in their culture. Although other types of folktales will be mentioned, I will concentrate on two specific groups of traditional stories, the trickster tale, a form popular throughout the region, and various Southeast Asian analogues of the equally popular Cinderella story. Chapter Three, The Coming of War, will discuss the painful and intensely traumatic transition from traditional life to refugee status. Chapter Four, A New World, will center on the difficult adjustment to life in the United States and other western nations and especially the pain of depression and post-traumatic stress disorder. Chapter Five, Memories and the Return Home, will discuss the small number of books which focus on the desire, sometimes realized, sometimes never more than a dream, but common to many Southeast Asian Americans, to revisit or return permanently to the home country. Refugees coming from Southeast Asia invariably bring a full load of their own emotional baggage with them, of course, but Chapter Six, Dealing with Racism, will concentrate on an issue that directly effects all Americans, the seemingly unavoidable human tendency to define those who are different as worthy of hatred. A number of the picture books under discussion attempt to offer age-appropriate solutions to this problem. In my conclusion I will examine some of the ideological issues dealt with in the books under consideration and the extent to which they can be used to help children of all ethnic backgrounds understand the Southeast Asian refugee experience.

Chapter One: Interpreting the Past

i

From the late-1960s well into the 1980s the primary images that most Americans had of Southeast Asia, garnered from *Life* magazine, the evening news, films like *Apocalypse Now* and *The Killing Fields,* or their own war-time experiences in Vietnam, were of monks burning themselves to death, executions carried out by means of a pistol shot to the head, firefights in Vietnam, or bodies lying in the killing fields of Cambodia. Later, due to the Vietnam War Memorial in Washington, D.C., films like *Born on the Fourth of July,* or in some cases personal experience, we became familiar with images of America's Vietnam War veterans, some of them seemingly so damaged by their experiences as to be unable to successfully reenter American society. These images haunt us to this day, and rightly so. Today, however, such images, rightly or wrongly are to some extent being replaced by happier or at least less emotionally-charged ones. American tourism of various sorts, not all of it entirely reputable, is a major growth industry in Thailand and, if Vietnam has not yet received "most favored" trade status, we are at least doing business with that nation. Still, images of war, devastation, and loss predominate in the popular culture, and children's literature is no exception. Whether we're talking about picture books or Young Adult novels, fiction or non-fiction, such works as Minfong Ho's *The Clay Marble* (1991), Sherry Garland's *The Lotus Seed* (1993), and Dia Cha's *Dia's Story Cloth* (1996) have become increasingly well known over the past decade as writers have attempted to interpret the Vietnam War and related conflicts for a new generation of young readers. Such works represent the majority of books we will be considering in this study.

There was, however, a time before the war in Vietnam and the related wars in Laos and Cambodia, and most of the children's books about refugees do at least make some reference to those earlier, better times. Further, a number of children's books about Southeast Asia, mostly folktales but also the occasional piece of historical fiction or non-fiction, are set in the pre-war period or at some earlier time which stands in strong and peaceful contrast to the war years. In order to better understand what was lost, it is worthwhile, I think, to take a detailed look at books that depict either the ancient past or the better times which immediately preceded the war years.

An issue which is always worth keeping in mind, however, when dealing with historical fiction or fiction set in a culture of which the writer is not a member concerns the accuracy of the information presented in the story, and this is a topic that we will be returning to on several occasions. The books under consideration in this study are essentially about underdogs. Regardless of the authors' attitudes towards the politics behind the wars in Vietnam, Laos, and Cambodia, no one writing for children on the subject of refugees is going to be hostile to the plight of people uprooted by violence and war. Especially, taking into account the fact that the majority of the writers are outsiders, though, people of something other than Southeast Asian heritage, and generally Americans, it seems likely that distortions of fact or nuance could easily creep into these stories. Characters and their actions may well be interpreted, intentionally or otherwise, in ways that are not entirely accurate but that make them more easily understood by American children, readers ignorant of the religious and ethnic traditions of the region. There may be a tendency to downplay what for many westerners would appear to be the negative aspects of the various traditional Southeast Asian cultures (arranged marriages, for example, or intensely patriarchal family structures which emphasize the importance of the group over the individual and the male over the female), a tendency to be, to use the currently popular phrase, "politically correct." Conversely, while not holding the refugees to blame for their plight, other writers may tend to tell their stories from what can only be called a pro-American perspective. Rightly or wrongly, such groups as the Khmer Rouge, the Pathet Lao and the Viet Cong will usually be portrayed as unalloyed villains. Indeed, although it can be inferred in several of the books under consideration, that a loved one, a lost parent, for example, has gone to war against the United States or that U.S. bombing raids are responsible for the death and destruction that made a book's protagonist a refugee, such embarrassing facts are rarely stated explicitly. Similarly, there will be a tendency to downplay some of the horrors faced by the books' protagonists even while describing them. Such a tendency exists in children's literature, of course, under any circumstances. Even writers of realistic fiction for young adults rarely try to convey the evils of our world in complete detail. Although the books under consideration in later chapters must perforce discuss the death, destruction, and degradation that is the lot of the refugee, none will go into it with the dedication to detail found in a film like *The Killing Fields* or a work of non-fiction for adults like JoAn D. Criddle's *To Destroy You Is No Loss.*

The point is this: although the writers whose books I am considering have generally tried to be as historically accurate as possible, their work, both fiction and non-fiction, being for children and largely having been written by outsiders, should not be seen as a perfect reflection of the historical facts. The events, those that occurred before, during, and after war time, may well be colored by the writers' own ideological perspectives, by their prejudices, or by their lack of knowledge of the finer nuances of Vietnamese, Cambodian, or Hmong culture (nuances which I also make no claim to understanding). Writing in 1981 Lai Nam Chen, in *Images of Southeast Asia in Children's Books*, decries the "meretricious images, such as racist stereotypes and cultural over-simplifications, that have been perpetuated in inferior books" (5) about Southeast Asia. In general such problems are less common in the more recent books I will be looking at, but it can't be denied that they may exist to some extent.

7

(Readers looking for more specific information on the ways in which Southeast Asian culture has been distorted in English-language children's literature would be well advised to read Chen's well-done, if somewhat dated study.) Further, when dealing with events before the war and particularly in the ancient past, there may well be a tendency to see the world through the proverbial rose-colored glasses. Even those books centered on the war itself or on the refugee experience after war, tend, quite understandably, to look to the past with sorrow and a certain nostalgia. Implicit in most of them is a longing for, to quote the title of Huynh Quang Nhuong's first memoir of his early life in Vietnam, *The Land I Lost*, a land no doubt made more beautiful and less difficult in memory simply by having been lost, both physically and due to the passage of time. Hindsight can be more accurate, but it also tends to wipe out inconvenient defects. This having been said, I would now like to turn to an examination of the Southeast Asian past, as presented in currently available children's books.

ii

While an increasing number of Vietnamese and Hmong refugee tales and folktales written explicitly for younger children in picture book form are appearing in bookstores and on library shelves, there is still little available in the way of well-written historical fiction, except, of course, to the extent that stories set at the time of the wars can now be seen as historical. For Cambodia, however, with its ancient high civilization this is not entirely the case. Inspired by the decorations on the twelfth-century temple at Angkor Wat, Jeanne M. Lee's lovely *Silent Lotus* (1991) tells the story of a little girl, born deaf, who never learns to speak. Friendless, except for the herons and cranes whose graceful gaits she learns to imitate, Lotus is at times terribly unhappy. Eventually, however, her parents decide to take her to the great temple in the city to ask the gods for help. The girl immediately begins to imitate the steps of the temple dancers, just as she has previously imitated the wading birds at home, and does so with such grace that the king and queen of Kampuchea enroll her in their dance pavilion. After much practice Lotus becomes the most famous dancer in the Khmer kingdom. Within the context of *Silent Lotus*, ancient Cambodia is seen as virtually utopian. Another Cambodian tale, *The Two Brothers* (1995), retold by Minfong Ho and Saphan Ros, concerns two penniless young brothers, both of whom become Buddhist monks, both of whom have been told that they are destined for great things. Leaving their monastery, Kem, the elder brother, travels to China as his abbot has commanded and becomes a wealthy merchant. The younger brother, Sem, however, less ambitious, fails to follow his abbot's advice. Marrying a pretty but shallow local girl, he settles down to a life of poverty. Years later, Sem goes looking for his brother to ask for help, unaware that his wife is fooling around behind his back. Receiving only minimal aid from Kem despite the latter's wealth, Sem returns home disappointed on one of his brother's junks. Sem has learned his lesson, however, and has determined to follow his abbot's advice at last. Staying alert, he catches a sea ogre in the act of abducting a sleeping sailor and, in classic fairytale fashion, wrings from it three magical gifts before he lets the monster go. When Sem returns home, his gifts are immediately stolen by his wife's boyfriend but, with the King's aid, the adulterous pair are soon punished. After the King annuls Sem's marriage the young man gives him the magical gifts. The King then marries Sem to his own daughter.

In both the straight historical tale, *Silent Lotus*, and the fairytale, *The Two Brothers*, the king of Cambodia acts as something of a *deus ex machina* by coming to the aid of humble people who have proven themselves worthy of his help through their accomplishments. Much the same is true in the Laotian trickster tale *Thao Kham, the Pebble Shooter*, retold by Cathy Spagnoli, which, like *Silent Lotus*, involves a poor, disabled child whose superior talents bring him to the King's attention. Thao Kham cannot walk, but he lives a good life in his humble village and gains many friends due to a peculiar talent. Thao Kham has the ability to shoot pebbles with unerring accuracy. This allows him to play a variety of tricks and eventually to develop a unique new art form. He shoots hundreds of holes into the giant leaves of an ancient banyan tree.

Each shot made a dot, a window for the sun. All the small holes then formed lines of light. Suddenly a green tiger ROARED into life. Like a shadow puppet, it moved in the wind, wondrous to watch (12).

Eventually his talent comes to the attention of the king who decides that Thao Kham is just what he needs to help him deal with a particularly garrulous advisor. The king stations the boy behind a curtain and has him shoot pebbles into the advisor's mouth whenever he opens it. Much pleased with the results of this trick, the king invites Thao Kham to stay in the palace on a permanent basis.

Much more somber, is the Hmong tale, *The Story of Mah* (1997), retold in picture book form by Rosalie Giacchino-Baker, and subtitled *A Hmong "Romeo and Juliet" Folktale.* This tale relates the story of a beautiful young Hmong woman named Mah who one day, while out gathering plants for yarn in the forest, meets Leu Xeng, a young man from the village north of the mountain. The couple soon fall in love, but their relationship comes to a bad end because Mah's family, who apparently don't know about Leu Xeng, have arranged a different husband for her. The two young people never consider marrying against their families' wishes, but Leu Xeng is so sad that he soon becomes ill and dies. Upon hearing of his death, Mah cries out "If we can't love each other in this world, we'll have to meet in another world" (22). Disconsolate, the young woman wanders off into the forest where she is soon found dead by her mother, through means unknown. Apparently recognizing the error of trying to force her daughter into an arranged marriage contrary to course of true love, the mother takes the blame for her daughter's death upon herself, and has her buried near Leu Xeng, "so the two of them could be together forever" (26). The tale has a *por quoi* ending; a hemp plant grows on Mah's grave and the girl's mother, taking this for a sign, transplants it into her garden. Later she weaves the hemp into cloth from which she makes a beautiful skirt of the sort that is now traditionally worn by Hmong brides.

The Story of Mah is told in an earnest, straightforward fashion by Giacchino-Baker who has strong credentials both as a specialist in multicultural education and as the author of several books about Southeast Asian literature, including a *Teacher's Resource Book for The Story of Mah,* which includes a variety of activities related to the tale along with some valuable background information on Hmong culture in general. The book is also beautifully illustrated by Lillian Shao who, we're told in a note, "spent many hours studying the textiles and folk art of the Hmong and working with Hmong consultants" (32) in order to perfect her art. Still, the grimness of the story, which puts it at odds with virtually all of the other narratives discussed in this chapter, makes it seem doubtful that the book will find much of an audience.

Published in 1963, Ruth Tooze's *Our Rice Village in Cambodia* is intended as contemporary non-fiction and indeed is dedicated to "Phuon and Neari," the two children who narrate the story. Tooze, however, explores a rural lifestyle that differs hardly at all from that of *Silent Lotus* or *The Two Brothers.* With a few minor adjustments in the details of the clothing in Ezra Jack Keats's illustrations, *Our Rice Village in Cambodia* could just as easily have been set in the nineteenth century, or perhaps even the twelfth century. The book involves a tour of what we are to assume is a typical Cambodian village. Phuon and Neari, who appear to be perhaps eight and six respectively, show us their house, built by their father from bamboo and palm leaves and raised on stilts, and their livestock living beneath. We're told that:

> Near our village are the rice fields,
> Where everyone works and plays,
> Where the good rice grows for us to eat—
> The rice, the good rice (19)

Keats's illustrations in green, black and white show an idyllic world of happy children, fat pigs, cleansing rains, hard working farmers and fishermen, beautiful river birds, singing, dancing and celebrations, all of which go to make up:

> My house, my family, my work, my play,
> Our village our friends, their work, their play,
> Water and rice and fish, daytime and nighttime,
> These make our life, our good life in Cambodia. (40)

This picture of Cambodian life is also similar to that found in the books of the

11

Vietnamese author Huynh Quang Nhuong which will be discussed later in this chapter. Intended for a very young audience, however, *Our Rice Village in Cambodia* omits all of the negatives associated with such an existence.

iii

Although non-fiction books about Southeast Asian refugees such as Muriel Stanek's *We Came from Vietnam* (1985), Diane Hoyt-Goldsmith's *Hoang Anh, A Vietnamese-American Boy* (1992) and Nancy Price Graff's *Where the River Runs, A Portrait of a Refugee Family* (1993) generally give some historical background, their emphasis is on the lives of Vietnamese and Cambodian refugee families in the United States and they will be dealt with in greater detail in Chapter Four. Straight non-fiction accounts of life in Vietnam and the rest of Southeast Asia prior to and since the wars written explicitly for younger children have also become fairly common in recent years.

Most recent non-fiction includes discussion of both traditional and contemporary Southeast Asian cultures but some of the books devote very little space to the great disruptions caused by the wars. Two series of note are Lerner Publications' *Journey Between Two Worlds* and Rosen Publishing's *Celebrating the People and Civilizations of Southeast Asia*. The latter, written on a third to fourth grade level (although accessible to advanced second graders), includes separate volumes, all by Dolly Brittan, on the people of Laos, Vietnam, Cambodia, Thailand, and the Philippines, as well as the Hmong. Lerner's superb series, which specifically focuses on refugees, also includes books about the Armenians, the Eritreans, the Kurds, the Tibetans, and other oppressed peoples as well as volumes on the Hmong and the Mien, an ethnic group closely related to, but separate from the Hmong, and is written on a fifth to sixth grade level. The Brittan texts, *The Hmong* (1997), *The People of Vietnam* (1998) and *The People of Cambodia* (1998), are divided into short chapters on history, language, religion, music, clothing, food and so forth with an emphasis almost entirely on the traditional cultures of Southeast Asia (The Hmong volume, for example, doesn't even mention the war). The excellent, but much more sophisticated Lerner volumes, *A Hmong Family* (1997) by Nora Murphy and *A Mien Family* (1996) by Sara Gogol, each center on a refugee family which emigrated to the United States and are unusual in that they devote considerable space not only to their subjects' wartime refugee experiences and their current American lives, but also discuss the pre-war history of the Hmong and Mien at some length. Similar in structure to the Brittan books, but written at a reading level comparable to the Lerner volumes, is The Lands, Peoples, and Cultures Series, created by Bobbie Kalman, which contains three volumes on Vietnam: *The Land* (1996), *The People* (1996), and *The Culture* (1996). Devoting most of their time to traditional Vietnamese culture none of the books in this series allots more than a paragraph to the war in Vietnam. All three series feature excellent color photographs, pronunciation guides, glossaries, maps, all the apparatus necessary to render the volumes reader friendly to elementary school children. Two series books for younger children that actually do discuss the wars in Southeast Asia at some length are *Laos* (1991), by Karen Jacobsen, a Children's Press *New True Book*, and *I Am Vietnamese American* (1997), by Felice Blanc, an *Our American Family* book. The former devotes two of its ten short chapters to the military conflicts in the region, beginning with the French occupation and moving into the 1980s (23-34). The latter devotes a short chapter apiece to Ho Chi Minh, The Vietnam War, and Refugees (9-13). *Laos* is unusual among books for younger children in that it also discusses the long-term conflicts between the various native peoples of the country, including the enslavement of one group, the Lao Theung, by another, the Lao Lum (15). More detailed, but again written for older children, are Sherry Garland's *Vietnam, Rebuilding a Nation* (1990) and Marybeth Lorbiecki *Children of Vietnam* (1997). Beautifully photographed by Paul P. Rome, Lorbiecki's book is one of the few works designed for children to mention Vietnam's ongoing problem, left over from the war, with landmines (33). Another valuable work of non-fiction for older children, Mace Goldfarb's *Fighters, Refugees, Immigrants, A Story of the Hmong* (1982) gives a detailed picture of life in a Thai relocation camp in the years immediately following the war in Vietnam as experienced by a volunteer

13

American doctor.

Virtually unique among histories of Southeast Asia for younger children is *Dia's Story Cloth, The Hmong People's Journey of Freedom* by Dia Cha, which is illustrated in its entirety by *pa'ndau*, the extraordinary Hmong art form that originated, in part, during their years in the Thai refugee camps. Writing in the first person, Cha narrates the story of the Hmong migration from China to Laos and other nations of Southeast Asia, briefly discusses the daily routine of Hmong life, and then concentrates on the war and its aftermath. Cha sees her own experience as emblematic of the catastrophic effect the war in Laos had on Hmong culture. Her father left to fight the communists, never to return, and later her village was attacked and destroyed. Eventually, after the Americans pulled out of Laos, Hmong families whose men had fought against the communists were forced to make a desperate and dangerous journey across the Mekong River to the relative safety of the Thai camps. Four and a half years later, Dia Cha and her family flew to the United States. Following Dia Cha's narration the book concludes with a more traditional historical essay by Joyce Herold, Curator of Ethnology at the Denver Museum of Natural History. For a more detailed account of traditional Hmong life in picture book form, however, there is also Ia Xiong's *The Gift The Hmong New Year*. One of the great concerns of the Hmong elders in America is that their children will grow up without adequate knowledge of their own traditional culture. *The Gift* is cast in the form of a fictional narrative about Dao, a little Hmong girl who is assigned by her American teacher to give a report on the culture of another country. Realizing that she knows very little about her own ethnic background, Dao asks advice from her mother who sends her to her grandfather Tong, a Laotian Hmong. The second half of the book is essentially the report Dao compiles based on her grandfather's stories. Although full of valuable information about traditional Hmong village life and dealing with an important topic, *The Gift*, unfortunately, is written in very flat language of a sort likely to diminish interest in the book.

Perhaps the most distinguished Vietnamese author of books for children in the

14

United States, Huynh Quang Nhuong, has produced two volumes of reminiscences, the award-winning *The Land I Lost, Adventures of a Boy in Vietnam* (1982) and *Water Buffalo Days, Growing Up in Vietnam* (1997). These chapter books, similar to Tooze's earlier *Our Rice Village in Cambodia*, but written at a fourth or fifth grade level in the author's own laconic, understated English, give a boy's eye view of life in a hamlet in the central highlands of Vietnam, a life filled with small pleasures and hard work. The two volumes overlap in some of their stories, indeed in a few cases the same sentences and even paragraphs appear in both books, and both volumes end with the coming of war, represented for the young Huynh Quang Nhuong by the death of his beloved water buffalo, Tank, who is hit by a stray bullet as French forces and Ho Chi Minh's Resistance exchange gunfire near his village. Few writers have done a better job than Huynh of describing day to day life in pre-war Southeast Asia, a way of life that ends suddenly and violently in the last chapter of each of his books.

The history of Southeast Asia, like the history of any part of our world, has its high points and its low points. There have been times of peace and times of chaos. War, however, has returned to the region again and again. In most of the historical fiction and narrative non-fiction for younger children that we have examined in this chapter, however, in *Silent Lotus, Thao Kham, Our Rice Village in Cambodia, or The Gift,* for example, the focus has tended to be on the child's immediate world and the events of a generally peaceful, almost edenic daily life. Problems have tended to be personal and have been dealt with individually. Power, as represented by parents (*The Story of Mah*) or the King (*Silent Lotus, Thao Kham, The Two Brothers*), has shown itself to be equally personal, and sometimes rather capricious. The straight historical works that we have looked at, those for younger children, through grade three at least, have tended either to eliminate all mention of warfare or to deal with it in a very brief space. Only in books for older children, such as Huynh Quang Nhuong's *The Land I Lost* and *Water Buffalo Days*, or in works that deal directly with the various wars in Southeast Asia, like Dia Cha's *Dia's Story Cloth* and Nora Murphy's *A*

Hmong Family, will young readers gain any real knowledge of the violent history of the region. Huynh Quang Nhuong's books seem particularly valuable in this regard because they sit so firmly on the dividing line between those edenic tales for small children, and works for older children that explore the violence inherent in the real world of Southeast Asia.

Chapter Two: The Way it Might Have Been

In this chapter I will be looking at a wide range of picture books that retell classic Southeast Asian folktales in English for a western audience. Several of the books discussed in Chapter 1, *The Two Brothers* and *The Story of Mah* for example, are also folktales, but I felt that it was worthwhile to consider them when I did because they exemplified certain general attitudes toward the past that were worth highlighting. In this chapter, I will concentrate on two sorts of traditional stories, trickster tales, many of which involve tricky animals (particularly rabbits and toads), and various Southeast Asian analogues of Cinderella.

i

Cambodia has a history of high civilization going back to ancient times, the Khmer empire having controlled much of Southeast Asia from the 9th through the 13th centuries. This classic grandeur is reflected, not only on the walls of Angkor Wat, but in such picture books as *Silent Lotus* and *The Two Brothers,* which were discussed in the previous chapter. Despite the centuries of chaos that followed the decay of the Khmer empire, however, despite the successive foreign powers which have conquered Cambodia, there is still in that country a long tradition of order and justice, perhaps not justice as it is practiced in modern democracies, but justice of the sort dispensed by Kings and their appointed judges. Typical of the Cambodian folktale are the stories of Judge Rabbit. Although he sometimes serves as a trickster in the folk literature of

Southeast Asia, much as he functions in African, African-American and Native American tales, in Cambodia Rabbit is frequently a figure of wisdom, a problem solver, someone to go to for answers. In Lina Mao Wall's retelling of the traditional tale *Judge Rabbit and the Tree Spirit,* for example, an evil spirit impersonates a woman's husband so that it may steal her away from him. When the real husband objects, the village judge, lacking the wisdom to deal with the situation, decrees that all three must live together. Judge Rabbit, however, when asked to help, plays a classic trick on the evil spirit by declaring that only the real husband can fit inside a small bottle.

The ending, of course, is obvious. Lina Mao Wall, herself a Cambodian refugee who has been the president of the Refugee Women's Alliance, writing in an afterward to her tale, says that hers is just "one of the many Judge Rabbit stories in our Cambodian folktale tradition. The character of Judge Rabbit shows healthy self-esteem and self-confidence. He believes in himself and his ability to solve problems...We tell the Judge Rabbit stories to our children at a very young age to encourage them to be self-confident, intelligent, gentle, kind and willing to help others out of their troubles. As Cambodian refugees, we see our children as our hope and our future" (32).

The Cambodian Judge Rabbit also appears in *Judge Rabbit Helps the Fish,* retold by professional storyteller Cathy Spagnoli, who has been instrumental in bringing many Southeast Asian folktales into print in the United States. Here the fish are in danger of extermination because the land animals have banded together to drain their pool and eat them all, but Judge Rabbit tricks the land creatures into sparing the lives of the fish by threatening them with the vengence of "Indrea, the Great Ruler" (24). Rabbit appears in a more traditional trickster guise in Minfong Ho and Saphan Ros's retelling of *Brother Rabbit, a Cambodian Tale,* in which the title character successively tricks a crocodile into taking him across a river, a woman into putting him into her basket so that he can eat her bananas, the crocodile again, an elephant into pulling him off a resinous tree stump where he's gotten his tail stuck, and the

18

crocodile for a third time. In this version Rabbit is entirely out for himself and cares very little for the needs of others. Ho and Ros write that "One of the recurring themes in Cambodian folktales is that of a small but quick-witted animal or person getting the better of someone stronger and meaner but not as bright. In Cambodian society, farmers and villagers saw themselves as small and weak compared to the powerful landlords, soldiers, and kings above them, and they reveled in stories in which the tables were turned" (np). They continue by noting that, despite the powerful Khmer empire, which at its height extended into present-day Thailand, Laos, and Vietnam, "Cambodia has often seen itself as the weaker nation among stronger, more aggressive neighbors....Like Brother Rabbit, the Cambodian people have remained irrepressible in the face of constant warfare, ready to rebuild their lives again through their quick wits and their resilience" (np). Yet another example of the weak but quick-witted hero tricking a powerful villain can be found in Alice Lucas's retelling of *How the Farmer Tricked the Evil Demon*, a traditional Cambodian tale recently published in an English/Hmong dual language edition by Pacific Asia Press. In this story a powerful demon repeatedly insists that a young farmer must give him half of his crops, but each time the monster explains which half he wants (for example, the part that grows underground, the part that grows above ground), the resourceful farmer comes up with a crop which will yield the demon nothing of value.

Such trickster characters are common throughout the folk literature of Southeast Asia and are being increasingly represented in English-language picture books. In Blia Xiong's version of *Nine-in-One, Grr! Grr!*, the first Hmong folktale made available in English-language picture book format, Tiger and her mate are lonely because they have no cubs, so she sets off to visit the great god or seer Shao (his exact nature varies depending on the version of the tale–see Johnson and Yang, xxvii) to ask him how many cubs she will have. Shao says that she will have "nine each year" (10), but only if she can remember his exact words. The prospect of having to deal with this many tigers upsets Bird who points out that "If Tiger has nine cubs each year, they will eat all of us. Soon there will be nothing but tigers in the land. You must change what you said, O Shao!" (20). Rather humble for so powerful a being, Shao admits his mistake, but cannot take back his promise. Fortunately, however, Bird is able to trick Tiger into thinking that Shao promised her only one baby in nine years. A similar concern for maintaining equilibrium in life is found in Cher Thao's *Only a Toad*, another traditional Hmong tale. Adapted by Brian and Heather Marchant in a bilingual format, this picture book concerns a toad who is depressed because he is "small and ugly and weak" (1). The toad therefore sets off on a journey "in hope of becoming a more powerful creature" (3). He successively imagines himself to be a pig, a dog, a farmer, and eventually a village mayor, each creature seemingly more powerful than the last. Eventually, however, some angry bees scare away the mayor and the toad, since he can eat the bees, realizes that his lot in life isn't so bad after all. Tiger appears as both trickster and fool in the Hmong traditional tale *Yer and the Tiger,* a sort of Southeast Asian Little Red Riding Hood. To the best of my knowledge this tale, although a popular subject for the Hmong *pa'ndau* story clothes (one of which hangs on the wall in the children's room of our local library), only exists in English-language children's book format in a version of the tale told by May Yang and more or less self-published by the noted translator of Hmong literature Charles R. Johnson, with simple, but well done illustrations by Danny Rodriquez. In this story Tiger kills a Hmong hunter and then decides to impersonate the man. The dead hunter's wife, oddly enough, can't tell the difference, but her little sister, Yer, can. She hides to avoid being eaten with the rest of the family and throws pepper in Tiger's eyes. She then convinces a bird to go to her brothers for help. When they show up, she tricks Tiger into thinking that they've come to negotiate her marriage to him, but, in a common motif, the brothers trap Tiger in a pit and kill him. Yer then returns home. Johnson also published a more sophisticated version of this tale, called "Sister-in-Law Nzeu and the Tiger: How a Brave Woman Won Out Over a Tiger," in his scholarly anthology *Myths, Legends and Folk Tales from the Hmong of Laos*, coedited with Se Yang. Yet another trickster tale, and something of an oddity, is Beverly Lewis's *Cows in the House*. Professionally produced, with colorful art by Chi

20

Chung, this traditional tale known in many cultures (one version involves a rabbi, for example), concerns a young boy who hates the noise generated by his family. When he goes to a wise man for help, the boy is told first to bring his cows into the house with him, then his cousins, and finally a wandering band of musicians. Eventually, at the wise man's suggestion, the boy throws all the extra people and animals out and finds the relative quiet that results from having only his immediate family present, quite restful. The book, published by Bethany House, a Christian press, is intended to illustrate Philippians 4:11, "For I have learned to be content with whatever I have." It is a delightful story, but I have reservations about its authenticity because, although Chung's illustrations appear to be intended to depict Hmong characters, the text itself never mentions the Hmong, only referring more generally to "a misty mountain village of Thailand" (4).

Toad, who appeared in Cher Thao's *Only a Toad*, also shows up in Jeanne M. Lee's retelling of the Vietnamese tale *Toad Is the Uncle of Heaven*. As in *Nine-in-One, Grr! Grr!*, the story begins with an animal who has a problem and who seeks redress from the gods. In this case there is a great drought and Toad, accompanied by Bees, Rooster, and Tiger, seeks the help of the King of Heaven. The King is angered when Toad accidentally jumps into His lap and attempts to punish the creature, but the King's various minions, including the royal Guards, the Thunder God, and the Hound of Heaven, are all foiled by the animals who have accompanied Toad. Deciding that he needs to treat the amphibian with more respect (hence the appellation "Uncle"), the King of Heaven promises to do Toad's bidding and make it rain. Now, whenever Toad croaks, the Vietnamese know that rain will follow. Yet another *por quoi* tale available in picture book format is Sherry Garland's retelling of the Vietnamese folktale *Why Ducks Sleep on One Leg*, which once again features animals who have a problem and decide to petition the Gods, in this case ducks who are unhappy because, as the book title suggests, they were created with only one leg each.

In contrast to the generally humorous stories discussed so far in this chapter is Aaron Shepard's beautifully written, and intensely romantic retelling of *The Crystal Heart, A Vietnamese Legend* (1998), which features lovely art by Joseph Daniel Fiedler. This story concerns Mi Nuong, the daughter of a great mandarin, who has been kept a virtual prisoner by her father for her entire life. One day, however, she hears the beautiful voice of a fisherman singing on the river below her tower. Although they've never met, Mi Nuong pines for her fisherman and seems close to death. When her father, the mandarin, finds the man and brings him to Mi Nuong, she realizes the inappropriateness of her love and is instantly cured. The fisherman, however, poor soul, now falls in love with her. Pining for the mandarin's daughter, he soon sickens and dies. When the people of his village discover his body, a large crystal of mysterious origin sits on his chest. They put both him and the crystal in his boat and allow it to float down the river. Finding the crystal and knowing nothing of its origin, the mandarin has it made into a teacup and presents it to his daughter. When Mi Nuong first attempts to drink from the cup, however, she sees the dead fisherman's face in her tea. Regretting her cruelty, Mi Nuong begins to cry and this frees the man's soul. Although she later marries the son of a great mandarin, Mi Nuong always regrets her lost fisherman.

What virtually all of the folktales discussed so far have in common is a concern for the underdog--helpless animals, poor farmers and fishermen, young lovers, the disabled. Frequently, when the tale has a happy ending, that happiness is brought about by an authority figure, a god, king, or wise judge. When a tale ends unhappily, as is the case in *The Story of Mah* or *The Crystal Heart*, it is because someone with power, a parent or a mandarin's daughter, has made a tragic mistake. Occasionally, however, as in the example of *Nine-in-One, Grr! Grr!* or *Toad Is the Uncle of Heaven*, such a mistake can corrected by a daring trickster.

ii

Although trickster tales are common in the folklore of Southeast Asia and are the type of folktale most widely available in English language picture books, the Vietnamese, Hmong, Cambodians and other peoples of the region have storytelling

22

traditions every bit as varied as those of Europe and elsewhere. Many of the more famous European folk and fairytales in fact have analogs among the traditional stories of Southeast Asia. Perhaps the best known of these is "Cinderella" and I would like to center the rest of this chapter on the several Southeast Asian versions of this story. Variants of this tale have been collected from virtually every country in the region. In fact, each ethnic group within a given country will frequently have its own version, or perhaps more than one. A number of studies have been done on the subject, most notably R. D. Jameson's classic essay "Cinderella in China" (1932) and, later, Nai-Tung Ting's full-length work *The Cinderella Cycle in China and Indo-China* (1974), however, virtually all of the extant scholarship has centered on the examination of these tales as folklore rather than as children's literature. My main purpose in this chapter is not to look at the original Southeast Asian versions of the Cinderella story, but rather to examine how those tales have been rendered into English for publication in the United States. To some extent these stories have been published with an eye toward various increasingly prominent (and increasingly English speaking) Southeast Asian communities within the U. S. To some extent they have been aimed at the traditional American children's book market, dominated, of course, by white middle-class kids and their parents. This has, at least in the view of various publishers, editors, translators, and "re-tellers," necessitated the introduction of a wide range of changes in the stories. It is these changes and the possible reasons behind them that I will be examining most carefully in this essay.

Although collections of Southeast Asian folk and fairytales have been available in English for many years, the sheer number of such volumes has increased considerably over the past decade. Among the best of these collections are *Folk Stories of the Hmong* (1991), compiled by Norma J. Livo and Dia Cha, *The Brocaded Slipper and Other Vietnamese Tales* (1992), edited by Lynette Dyer Vuong, Vuong's *The Golden Carp and Other Tales from Vietnam* (1993), *Thai Tales* (1994), retold by Supaporn Vathanaprida, and the bi-lingual *Stories from Laos*, edited by Rosalie Giacchino-Baker, which includes Lao, Hmong, Khammu, and Iu-Mien tales. The current interest in the many variants of "Cinderella" has also led to the recent publication of a number of such Southeast Asian tales in picture book form. It is these picture book versions of the story, beginning with Darrell Lum's retelling of *The Golden Slipper*, that I want to examine in detail.

The Golden Slipper is a Vietnamese Cinderella and, like most of the other Southeast Asian variants that will be discussed here, is clearly descended from what Marina Warner calls "the earliest extant version of `Cinderella' to feature a lost slipper" (202), the Chinese tale of Yeh-hsien. As in the European version of the story, the heroine, known as Tam, is mistreated by her stepmother, who badly spoils her own younger daughter, Cam, and, of course, things get worse after Tam's father, a poor rice farmer, dies. One day, at Cam's insistence, the girls go to catch prawns. Tam works hard and is successful while Cam spends the day playing. The younger girl tricks the older, however, and steals Tam's prawns. Crying for her long-lost mother, Tam is surprised to find herself confronted by "a beautiful woman dressed in royal colors" who comforts her and calls her a princess. Advising Tam to "listen to the animals that surround" her, the woman disappears, leaving behind a small golden catfish which the girl takes home and deposits in the local pond. She feeds the catfish daily and also is kind to the family's rooster and horse. Eventually it is time for the Autumn Festival. As one might expect, Tam's wicked stepmother finds the money to dress her own daughter in silk in the hope of attracting the prince's attention at the festival, but tells Tam that she can only go if she first husks an entire cartload of rice. Because of her kindness to the animals, though, they, along with the mysterious woman from the pond, help Tam finish her work and provide her with beautiful and magical clothing, including a pair of "golden brocade slippers." In a reversal of the pattern set by the European Cinderella, however, Tam loses her slipper on the way to the festival. Finding it, the prince is impressed by its beauty and wants to meet the slipper's owner. All the young women attempt to claim it but only Tam can wear the slipper and the prince immediately falls in love with her. They're soon married and the stepmother and stepsister retire to a life of frustration and poverty.

24

Another Vietnamese version of Cinderella is available in Lynette Dyer Vuong's collection *The Brocaded Slipper and Other Vietnamese Tales*. Written for an audience of somewhat older children than Lum's version of the story, "The Brocaded Slipper," changes a number of minor details and greatly elaborates and extends the plot. Cam is not just younger than Tam, but specifically ugly and lazy. They are sent to the pond to catch fish rather than prawns and Cam steals her stepsister's catch because her mother has promised a new blouse to the girl who brings back the most fish. When the beautiful woman appears, she is specifically identified as a "fairy." The largest difference between the two stories, however, involves the magic fish. In this version of the tale Cam finds out about it, spears the fish and eats it for lunch. At the fairy's direction, Tam finds the fish's bones, and buries them. Three months later she digs them up and finds that the bones have transmuted into beautiful clothing, including a pair of brocaded slippers. A crow almost immediately steals one of her slippers, carries it to the capital, and drops it at the prince's feet. He assumes the slipper must belong to a beautiful princess and falls in love with her sight unseen. From here "The Brocaded Slipper" parallels the European Cinderella fairly closely. The king, who wants his son wed in any case, proclaims a huge celebration and all the young women of the kingdom are invited to try on the slipper. The wicked stepmother hurries her ugly daughter off to the affair, telling Tam she can come only after she finishes sorting an enormous number of sesame seeds. Tam receives magical help from the animals, puts on the beautiful clothes she's kept hidden, and hurries to the celebration. The only young woman who can wear the brocaded slipper, she soon marries the prince.

At this point, however, where many versions of Cinderella end, "The Brocaded Slipper" is still gathering steam. Tam's wicked stepmother tricks her into climbing a tree to gather nuts and then cuts it down. Tam is killed in the fall and her spirit flies off in the form of an oriole. Faking sorrow, the stepmother informs the prince of Tam's death and offers him Cam as a substitute. The two are soon wed though the marriage doesn't flourish. Then Tam returns to the prince in her bird form and Cam finds herself ignored. Overcome by jealousy, she kills the bird and eats it, burying the bones. You can't keep a good heroine down, however, and Tam returns again, this time as a pair of peach trees. Again overcome by jealousy Cam has the trees cut down and their wood turned into a loom, but its noise carries the sound of Tam's voice and drives the wicked stepsister to distraction. Tam also returns as a persimmon and then as the daughter of a poor woman. Needless to say, the prince soon stops at the poor woman's house, recognizes Tam through her ability to flawlessly prepare betel leaves for chewing, and brings her home. Cam, the wicked stepsister, dies while attempting to flee the palace, but everyone else lives happily ever after.

It's difficult to know the extent to which either the Darrell Lum or the Lynette Dyer Vuong versions of the tale are authentically Vietnamese, as opposed to being influenced by European and specifically French versions of Cinderella. In compiling her book, however, it should be noted that Vuong did consult a number of earlier volumes of folktales assembled by Vietnamese collectors which she lists in her Introduction. An interesting comparison can be made between these two Vietnamese Cinderellas and the similar tale of *Jouanah*, which comes from the Hmong oral tradition. Adapted by Jewell Reinhart Coburn with Tzexa Cherta Lee and published in the United States both an English-language version and a Hmong-language version (as *Ntsuag Nos, Ib Tug Cinderella Hmoob*), both volumes feature the art of Anne Sibley O'Brien. In a Publisher's Note Coburn makes clear the impossibility of defining any one variant of such a tale as "the" authentic version. She writes:

> This centuries-old folktale was introduced to us by Blong Xiong in a story entitled "The Poor Girl." Another version of the story, "Ngao Nao and Shee Na" can be found in *Folk Stories of the Hmong* by Norma J. Livo and Dia Cha. We based the story of Jouanah on these sources as well as the oral traditions from Tzexa Cherta Lee's family.

It is also noted that the illustrator went to great lengths to achieve authenticity. The clothing shown in *Jouanah,* based on photographs, videos and actual attire, is specifically that of the Blue Hmong, an ethnic subdivision that most American readers

26

of the book won't even be aware of, but which is of great importance to the Hmong themselves. I mention this only because a Hmong-American teacher's aide who attended a presentation I gave on Southeast Asian children's literature last year was troubled by the book's illustrations. She was White Hmong and had always envisioned the tale in terms of her own specific cultural background.

Jouanah, which means "young orphan," begins very differently from other Cinderella stories. It concerns a farmer and his wife who have gone to the market to buy a cow. Having failed to find an appropriate animal, the wife says "We must have a cow to plow our fields and carry the grain...Let me become a cow for awhile to help bring in the crops." The husband apparently knows exactly what magic is needed to turn his wife into a cow and does so on the spot. When he brings her home, his daughter, Jouanah, is understandably upset but, with the cow helping, the farm soon prospers. The greedy farmer, however, refuses to turn the cow back into his wife. Instead he remarries. The new stepmother resents the cow (who has the magical ability to spin silken thread on her horns) and immediately takes a dislike to Jouanah because she is more beautiful than the woman's own daughter, Ding. Terrorizing both her new husband and Jouanah, the stepmother makes them both work like dogs. She also pretends to be a tree spirit and tricks the farmer first into burning Jouanah's silk thread and then into agreeing to kill the cow. He's spared this murder, however, because the cow immediately dies of a broken heart, and the father follows soon thereafter. When the New Year arrives, the wicked stepmother and her daughter hurry off to the celebration, which will last several days, leaving Jouanah not just to clean the rice, but with orders to remove thousands of small stones that have maliciously been stirred into it. Two days later, having finished her chore, the girl reaches for her mother's sewing basket, in which she has hidden a piece of the dead cow's hide. Beneath it, miraculously, she finds a complete set of beautiful clothes, including a headdress, two purses bordered with coins, an elaborate silver necklace, and, of course, a dainty pair of shoes. Guided by her mother's voice, Jouanah dresses and hurries to the festival where she catches the eye of Shee-Nang, the son of the

27

village Elder, a "fine young man of learning and wealth" who also plays the Hmong *qeng* and dances with great skill[1]. Shee-Nang has eyes only for Jouanah, who nobody recognizes of course, but she leaves hastily, losing one of her shoes. He goes searching for her, carrying the shoe from house to house in the traditional manner. In an odd variation, Jouanah doesn't try on the shoe because her stepmother forbids it, but Shee-Nang can tell at a glance that it will fit anyway. Needless to say the couple are soon wed, leaving Jouanah's stepmother and stepsister "plotting and scheming, making endless misery for only themselves." The magical piece of cowhide lies safely hidden in the old sewing basket, ready to provide aid for Jouanah's children and their children after them.

Coburn mentions that she has made a minor change in the name of her protagonist "in order to make the name more accessible to an American audience." A glance at "Ngao Nao and Shee Na" the Cinderella variant found in Livo and Cha's *Folk Stories of the Hmong*, which was one of Coburn's sources, however, makes it seem probable that other changes were also introduced, not just to make the story more accessible, but also to make it more palatable to an American audience. This can be a dangerous procedure for, as Lai Nam Chen points out in *Images of Southeast Asia in Children's Books*, "when a reteller does not approach cultural differences in such matters with enough seriousness, but instead overrides them in the facile assumption that all folktale variants are as penetrable to the Western mind as Asian costumes and artifacts, he, unwittingly perhaps, distorts the tale and Westernizes it" (14). As retold by Livo and Cha, in a volume that very definitely is not intended for young children and that it is probably much more authentic than the picture book versions of the tale, there is no stepmother. Rather there are two wives simultaneously (93), each of whom has a daughter. When the second (and lesser) wife gets sick it is because the husband has never performed the required sacrifice of a cow for his dead parents and a shaman tells the family that they must now do so. Unable to find a cow,

---

[1]The ability to play the *queng*, an elaborate instrument made from bamboo *while* dancing is a skill much prized in Hmong culture and appears repeatedly in folktales as proof of a young man's excellence.

however, the husband magically transforms his healthy first wife into one without her permission. The second wife quickly becomes a tyrant, mistreating the daughter of the former first wife, in this variant named Ngao Nao[2]. As a cow, the mother helps her daughter with her weaving, but refuses to help Ngao Sang (whose name translates as "young sly one"), the daughter of the second wife. Angered by this, the second wife demands that the cow finally be sacrificed, but the man hesitates. Pretending to be sick again, the second wife tricks the man much as Jouanah's stepmother did in Coburn's version of the tale, and convinces him to kill the cow immediately. The cow, however, chooses to commit suicide by intentionally falling on a knife (96). The family cooks and eats the dead animal, thereby committing cannibalism of a sort (96), all except Ngao Nao, who places her portion of the meat in the cow's food trough where it is magically transformed into new clothes. These she wears to the New Year's festival after performing the requisite separation of the rice grains from the chaff. Ngao Nao's romance with Shee Na (whose name translates as "quick as a snake") is pretty much unchanged from the Coburn version of the story. Oddly though, it is noted that Shee Na, the handsome young man, spits while he dances and plays the *qeng* (like a French horn player, perhaps), and Ngao Sang's wicked mother tells her "to kiss the spit wherever it fell" (97). Shee Na also emerges as something of a trickster in this version of the tale, playing several tricks on the second wife and her daughter. Further, there is no mention of a lost shoe, the happy couple sleep together on the night *before* they get married and they almost immediately have a child. Coburn's version of the tale ends with the marriage, but the Livo and Cha version continues, somewhat in the manner of the extended Vietnamese variant summarized above, with a further tale of murder and mayhem. Angered by her failure to wed Shee Na, the wicked Ngao Sang kills the good Ngao Nao with a knife and then tries unsuccessfully to usurp her place as wife and mother. Later Ngao Nao reappears without explanation, the daughter of a different mother, but still wearing Shee Na's ring and the couple is reunited.

---

[2] "Ngao Nao" (young orphan) and "Jouanah" are actually the exact same word written under two different systems by which the Hmong oral language is rendered into our alphabet.

Eventually Ngao Nao, the Cinderella figure in this decidedly un-western version of the story, takes revenge on Ngao Sang by pushing her into a wok full of boiling water and then dismembering her body. Ngao Sang's wicked mother is outraged by her daughter's death, which she discovers because Ngao Nao has placed parts of the dead daughter's body in the mother's basket. The mother

> was furious and wanted revenge. She wished they were both dead. She wished so hard that her wishes came true. Shee Na changed into a tree and Ngao Nao became a beehive. Their son turned into a bird (100).

Assuming that the original version of the tale that Coburn was working with was similar to "Ngao Nao and Shee Na" it is, perhaps, easy to understand why she chose to make the changes and cuts that she did! In yet another version of the tale, identified by R. D. Jameson as simply "Annamite," the protagonist, Medea-like, specifically feeds the dead girl's flesh to her stepmother (80).

Just published in 1998, Coburn's retelling of *Angkat: the Cambodian Cinderella*, is actually based on a tale found in an essay entitled "Le Conte de Cendrillo Ches Les Cham" by the eighteenth-century French folklorist Adhemard Leclére, so its Southeast Asian authenticity is clearly suspect. Coburn notes, however, that she was aided in her adaptation of the tale into English by Riem Men, a Cambodian educator. The tale she insists "upholds the traditional Khmer values of duty, loyalty, and perseverance which are also prevalent in Cinderella's European versions." Angkat, by the way, means "child of ashes." In this variant the heroine is the daughter of a widowed fisherman and is described as "dutiful and obedient...the joy of her father's life." The fisherman soon remarries a widow who has a daughter who is "a girl of great beauty," but with "no redeeming qualities." Unlike most of the Cinderellas of either European or Southeast Asian provenance, however, Angkat protests loudly when her stepsister is officially awarded the right to be called Number One daughter and there is little peace in the family. The stepmother sets up a fishing contest for the right to that title. A cocky girl, our heroine Angkat, who likes to fish, expects to win, especially since her stepsister is lazy. Of course, when, exhausted from hard work, she takes a nap, and her stepsister steals all of her fish but one and wins the title. Dejected, Angkat assumes that her other fish have simply escaped and releases the one she has left into her father's pond. Not realizing that she's been cheated, she accepts the role of Number Two daughter and takes on all of the household chores. Her remaining fish, of course, turns out to be magical and brings her much pleasure until her jealous stepsister secretly catches and eats it. Heartbroken at the disappearance of her pet, Angkat is comforted by the god-like, no doubt Buddhism-inspired Spirit of Virtue who counsels her to place the fish's bones under her mat with predictable results, "two dainty, golden slippers." The Spirit also counsels her to put one of her new slippers by the window where it is soon stolen by a "mystical" bird and brought to the prince. It's interesting to note that, although the bird who takes the slipper appears in early Egyptian versions of the tale, it does not appear in the best known Chinese variant, Yeh-Shen.

As in "The Brocaded Slipper" the prince decides to marry the owner of the footgear without having ever met her. Hurrying to the celebration where all the young women will be trying on the slipper, Angkat's wicked stepmother scatters rice over a nearby field, telling her she must collect every grain before she can attend. Helped by chickens, she does this quickly, changes her clothes, and speeds to the palace where things go pretty much as one might expect and the couple is soon wed. In the Vietnamese versions of the tale, like most European versions, Tam's father died soon after marrying the stepmother, but in the Cambodian variant the father is still alive and readily agrees to the stepmother's plot to murder the newly married Angkat, crushing her under an enormous soup pot. As in the Vietnamese version of the story, the prince, heartbroken, thinking Angkat's death an accident, agrees to marry the stepsister. Soon, however, Angkat's spirit returns, first in the form of a banana plant, then as bamboo. One day, while hunting, the prince enters the bamboo grove and its rustling reminds him of his dead wife. Ordering the grove transplanted to his palace, he spends most of his time there and eventually Angkat appears in the flesh. The wicked fisherman, his wife and stepdaughter are all banished from the land and everyone lives happily ever after.

The similarities between the several Southeast-Asian picture book versions of Cinderella are many and complex. Equally intricate are the correspondences between them and the various formerly little known African, East Asian, Native American, Middle Eastern and European variants of the tale that have appeared in picture book form in recent years (not to mention the familiar Perrault and somewhat less familiar Grimm versions of the story). Without examining more clearly traditional variants of the Southeast-Asian tales in their original languages, of course, it is impossible to know with absolute certainty the extent to which the similarities actually existed in the originals as opposed to having been added by "retellers" like Coburn, Lum and Vuong in order to make them more acceptable to a western audience. It seems clear, however, simply from the Livo and Cha version of "Ngao Nao and Shee Na" already examined, that, as is sometimes the case with the tales of the Brothers Grimm (including Aschenputtel, their version of Cinderella), more traditional Southeast Asian variants of the story may not be deemed entirely suitable for presentation to small children in picture book form without heavy editing and rewriting.

Of greatest interest, perhaps, are the differences between the Southeast Asian Cinderellas and the versions of the story with which westerners are most familiar. For example, in all of the Vietnamese, Hmong and Cambodian variants of the tale, it's clear that the parents of the main character, whether they be farmers or fisherfolk, are peasants, people of humble status. More often than not they are specifically poor. In the western versions of the story, however, Cinderella's parents are almost invariably gentry. In the A.E. Johnson translation of Perrault, which features the classic illustrations of W. Heath Robinson, Cinderella's father is "a worthy man" (58) and his high status is emphasized when we learn that only "persons of high degree" have been invited to the ball (60). In Marcia Brown's Caldecott Award-winning "free translation" the father is called a "gentleman" and the ball invitation goes out to "everyone who was anyone." In the Padraic Colum edition of *Grimm's Fairytales* we're specifically told that Aschenputtel's father was "a rich man" (121) and other translations of both

Perrault and the Brothers Grimm describe the family in a similar manner. Because the traditional Vietnamese and Cambodian cultures never developed a full-fledged gentry class, however, the division between haves and have nots tended to be even more absolute than in pre-modern Europe. The Hmong, on the other hand, are a tribal culture and have no real tradition of kingship or a noble class, so the fine young man Jouanah marries is simply the son of the village elder or, in the Livo and Cha version nothing more than "a handsome young man" (96) with well-developed musical skills. Oddly though, the Hmong variant of Cinderella, "Ngao Nao and Shee Na" has a sequel, which also exists in several versions. In one, the king of a distant country falls in love with Ngao Nao after seeing one strand of her hair (which had floated down river after she washed it) and forces Shee Na to trade her for the king's seven wives (Johnson and Johnson, 81). In another version, the king falls in love with her portrait and simply takes the young woman by force (Johnson and Yang, 346-47).

Another major difference between the eastern and western versions of the tale can be found in the events that immediately lead up to and follow the marriage of the Cinderella character and the eventual fate of the wicked stepmother and stepsister(s). In Brown's version of Perrault the stepsisters simply can't fit the glass slipper on their feet. Later, after she marries the prince, Cinderella, a good Christian (and a tad co-dependent, perhaps), "embraced them and told them she forgave them with all her heart. She begged them to love her always." In the Johnson translation of Perrault, she goes even further, forgiving and pardoning them, asking them to love her, and then "setting aside apartments in the palace for her two sisters and marry[ing] them the very same day to two gentleman of high rank about the court" (68). Written for a German middle-class that was less ethereal and perhaps less willing to do the noble thing than was Perrault's more courtly audience, the Grimm brothers' "Aschenputtel" includes a variety of gruesome touches which brings it closer to what are probably the more authentic Asian versions of the tale. The stepsisters each cut off part of a foot in an attempt to get into the glass slipper and might have gotten away with their deception if the prince, who is fooled by each mutilation in turn, isn't warned of the

33

deception by a pair of magical singing pigeons (126-27). Then, after the wedding, when the "two false sisters came and wanted to get into favor with Cinderella and share her good fortune," the pigeons, shades of Hitchcock's *The Birds*, peck out their eyes (127-28). Even the violent events that occur in the Grimm's tale, however, pale in comparison to those found in the more obviously traditional Southeast Asian versions of the story mentioned above.

Also of interest in the Vietnamese, Cambodian and Hmong variants, as one might expect in cultures influenced to various degrees by Buddhist, Hindu, and animist religions, is the emphasis on both the continued presence of the dead and reincarnation. In these stories, called "spirit tales" by Jenkins and Austin (185), death simply doesn't end things. In Coburn's *Jouanah*, the girl's mother, having first been transformed into a cow and then died of sorrow prior to being murdered, is still around as a spirit at the end of the story to watch over Jouanah and her children. This can be seen, perhaps, as parallel to Aschenputtel's dying mother's promise, at the beginning of the Grimm's variant of the tale that "I will look down on you from heaven and be near you" (121). Cinderella's fairy godmother, of course, is, at least in part, a product of Perrault's imagination and doesn't exist in the Grimm's version of the story. In the Grimm's tale Aschenputtel receives magical aid from various birds, in a manner similar to some of the Asian versions of the story, and specifically from birds who roost in a tree immediately above her dead mother's grave. In Coburn's Cambodian variant, *Angkat*, Vuong's Vietnamese version, and the Livo and Cha retelling of the Hmong tale, the Cinderella character is murdered, but comes back to life in order to be reunited with her husband and, incidentally, punish the wicked. So far as I'm aware Cinderella does not die in any European version of the story. The pigeons who clue the prince in to the wicked stepsisters' attempt to fit into the glass slipper by cutting off parts of their feet may, perhaps, be seen as a reincarnation of the the dead mother, of course, if only on a symbolic level. A similar voice from beyond the grave motif can be found in the classic medieval ballad, "The Twa Sisters" (Child, 128).

Specialists in post-colonial studies are quick to point out the problems that can occur whenever writers attempt to deal with cultures not their own. Numerous papers and books on this subject have appeared in recent years deconstructing the work of everyone from Shakespeare to Kipling to Doris Lessing and this is also a serious concern within the realm of children literature. Contemporary children's authors almost invariably do their best to be accurate (although there are a few glaring exceptions--witness Susan Jeffers's well-known *Brother Eagle, Sister Sky: A Message from Chief Seattle* (1991), which, despite its beauty and its positive environmental message, has been widely criticized for its visual and textual inaccuracies[3]). Still, the controversies are numerous and questions are frequently asked by critics, teachers, librarians and parents. Do the events narrated in a book accurately reflect the history of the culture? In the case of traditional literature, are the thoughts, beliefs, and actions of the characters being reinterpreted to fit western norms? To what extent are western authors guilty of what is sometimes called "appropriation" or cultural poaching, in effect stealing or co-opting the stories of less affluent cultures? Should an author even try to write about characters from a culture other than his or her own? Many readers may consider such questions irrelevant, petty, or actively obnoxious, particularly if they're primarily interested in simply reading a good story or presenting one to children, but others consider such issues enormously important. Even as I write this paragraph an extended and occasionally heated exchange is taking place between various experts on the Children's Literature listserve concerning the accuracy of Suzanne Fisher Staples's *Shabanu* (1989), an award-winning YA novel about life in contemporary Pakistan. Similar arguments have occurred on the listserve in recent months about works as diverse as Jeffers's *Brother Eagle, Sister Sky*, Jane Yolen's *Encounter* (1992), and the two recent retellings of "Little Black Sambo."

Our examination of the various Southeast Asian versions of the Cinderella

---

[3] See, for example, Fergus M. Bordewich, *Killing the White Man's Indian*. New York: Doubleday, 1996, pp. 132-3.

story, however, makes it obvious that such issues are relevant even within the context of the fairytale, a genre seemingly far removed from contemporary controversy. There is reason to believe that Coburn and the other retellers are intentionally rewriting the traditional tales in ways that may not be entirely accurate but that do make them more easily understandable for American children, readers ignorant of the religious and ethnic traditions of Southeast Asia. This is accomplished in part by emphasizing the similarities between the Asian stories and their European analogs and in part by downplaying or in a few cases even eliminating those elements of the tales that some westerners might find offensive, including such things as polygamy, premarital sex, reincarnation, or the heroine's taking active and violent revenge upon those who have done her wrong. Are such changes appropriate? Do they violate the spirit of the tales? Are they unfair to the cultures which produced the stories?

Obviously there is no single correct answer to these questions. It's hard to criticize anyone for trying to make difficult material accessible to children and the impulse towards cultural diversity behind the recent increase in the availability of children's picture books based on Southeast Asian stories is clearly something to be lauded. Nor is it easy to criticize the tendency represented by these books to emphasize similarities between diverse people. In a late-twentieth/early twenty-first century America still troubled by ethnic strife and the apparent unwillingness of many European Americans to accept the importance of the cultural contributions of Americans of non-European heritage, it would seem to behoove us as critics and educators to support what might be called the "It's a Small World After All" impulse. On the other hand, living as I do in a small Midwestern city which was once almost entirely Caucasian, but which has in recent years had to adapt itself to the presence of an increasingly significant number of Southeast Asian immigrants, Hmong Americans in our case, I have become acutely aware that our tendency to try and achieve positive relationships by ignoring differences can cause as many problems as it solves. Cultures do differ in what they see as morally acceptable behavior and sometimes those differences are dramatic. The Hmong of Wisconsin are hard

36

working, intelligent people who have done a remarkable job of fitting into a culture that is radically different from their own. Too often, however, we have tried to minimize their differences and thus have been caught by surprise when problems occurred. We have thus tended to ignore Hmong traditions that Americans do not approve of (child marriage and the ritual kidnapping of brides, for example) until there was a crisis and then defined such behavior as criminal. We may also, I think, have tended to misunderstand certain traditional forms of association that have led in America to the formation of Hmong youth gangs.

The subject of youth gangs brings us a fair distance away from "Cinderella," of course, but there is a connection. By attempting to westernize the traditional literature of a different culture, even when those stories have obvious connections to our own literature, we run the very real risk of distorting and misunderstanding that culture. If the point of reading a fairytale is simply to enjoy it for itself, this is not a difficulty. If the point, however, at least in part, is to use the story as a way of understanding how the people of that culture might think about the truly important issues that are at the heart of most fairytales, than perhaps it is a problem. "Cinderella," for all of its apparent distance from our world, does deal with important issues. It's about children's fear of losing a parent and of losing their place in the family. It's about having an appropriate relationship with the natural (and, for that matter, the supernatural) world. It's about the importance of doing what's right despite the difficulties that might ensue. And, finally, it's also about acceptable female behavior and what girls can and should do to take control of their own lives. These are universal issues, of course, but they aren't issues about which all cultures agree. A case in point to end this chapter: despite western stereotypes concerning Asian attitudes towards women, the heroines of the least westernized Southeast Asian versions of Cinderella, tend to be the most feisty. It's hard to imagine the co-dependent Cinderella of Perrault, the passive beauty of Walt Disney, or any other western Cinderella (prior, of course, to Drew Barrymore in *Ever After* (1998)) having the nerve to stand up to her step-sister and step-mother, let alone take up an edged weapon in her own defense.

Chapter Three: The Coming of War

Traditionally, whether in folktales or in real life, Americans have tended to root for the underdog. It was, therefore, one of the great ironies of the United States's involvement in Southeast Asia that we found ourselves, for whatever reasons, good or bad, in the position normally associated with the bully. We were, in effect, Goliath fighting a North Vietnamese David. Virtually all of the children's books that deal with the war in Vietnam from the viewpoint of the native people of Southeast Asia are in fact tales of little people, underdogs--farmers and villagers for the most part. In some cases the underdogs fight back against their aggressors, but more often than not they are simply caught in the crossfire and forced to flee their homes. And much the same is true in children's books published about the Hmong and the Cambodians.

The next type of story we will be looking at, therefore, covers the great transition from the traditional, generally rural lifestyle of Southeast Asia to refugee status. Usually told from the child's perspective, such stories follow all or some segments of a fairly predictable pattern. First, there are rumors of war, then the father of the family leaves or is taken away to become a soldier. Eventually, perhaps years later, guns are heard in the distance and then the war comes to the child's village, forcing him or her to flee with some fragment of the remaining family. A harrowing journey must be made by airlift, or through the jungle, or across the Mekong River, or over some part of the South China Sea. Grandparents die enroute. Eventually the survivors reach an internment camp where, after enduring months, sometimes years, of privation and intense boredom punctuated by the occasional danger of enemy attacks from across the border, they eventually receive permission to travel to the United States, Australia, or elsewhere.

Once again, most of the books under consideration in this chapter begin with either rumors or the direct experience of war. For the Vietnamese, of course, war has sadly been a way of life for many decades, but immigration to the United States didn't begin in earnest until the early to mid-1970s. Most of these immigrants were well educated: university students, the wives of U.S. servicemen, and Vietnamese government officials (Rutledge, 16). The first great wave of immigration to the United States, however, occurred in 1975, immediately following the fall of Saigon. Included in this group, most of whom were airlifted, were large numbers of Vietnamese government and military personnel, others who had collaborated with the United States, and their families. A second wave of immigration occurred in the late 1970s, largely in response to the resettlement policies of the new Communist government in Vietnam. Most of these people travelled by boat and a high percentage of them were less well-educated farmers and fishermen (Rutledge, 24). The Hmong, many of whom fought for the U.S. government as part of the secret war in Laos, first began reaching America in 1976, generally after spending time, sometimes years, in resettlement camps in Thailand. They continue to immigrate to the U.S. to this day (Cha, Afterword, np), although it has been estimated that approximately one-third of the 300,000 Hmong who lived in Laos in the 1970s died in the war or its aftermath (Johnson and Yang, vii). Cambodians were directly and adversely affected by the Vietnam War, but the worst damage to that country occurred in and after 1975 at the hands of their own, native-bred revolutionaries, the Khmer Rouge. In that year the communist dictator Pol Pot put into effect policies which over the next decade killed some three and a half million of his own people (Graff, 49). Cambodians began to flee their country in the mid-1970s, most of them ending up in Thai resettlement camps. Immigration to the U.S. began a few years later and, again, continues to this day.

Anyone who reads these books will gain a number of immediate impressions.

First, regardless of the ethnic background of the characters, the books, particularly those aimed at younger children, actually give very little detail about the wars involved, or at least very little in the way of what might be called "proper noun" detail. When the Vietnamese protagonist of Garland's *The Lotus Seed* must flee for her life because "One day bombs fell all around and soldiers clamored door to door" (np), we are never told which side the soldiers are on and Tatsuro Kiuchi's illustration for the text simply shows civilians running against a background of burning buildings and smoke blackened skies. Prior to this we have only been told that her husband had "marched off to war," presumably never to return because she has had to raise her children alone. For the Vietnamese children of Rosemary Breckler's *Sweet Dried Apples,* despite the fact that their father has left home to fight, the war is little more than a distant annoyance, a half-heard rumbling in the background that accompanies their games, until one day it takes away their beloved grandfather and destroys their homes and fields. That the "enemy" is American bombers using napalm is implicit in both the text and in Deborah Kogan Ray's highly abstract illustration, but never specifically stated.   We're simply told that

> The night suddenly became bright with fire. Everything around us seemed to be burning....
> In the morning, we crawled out to a black world. The bamboo trees were gone. All around us were mountains that we had never seen. No birds sang in the sky. The rice fields were ashes. We all wept (np).

Chong, the Hmong protagonist of Brian and Heather Marchant's *A Boy Named Chong,* like the children who narrate most of these books, lived a happy life "in the hilltops of Laos, Where I lived in grandfather's house....Until shots in the village were heard" (4-6). The illustrations, by Ya Lee, of life prior to the war are idyllic, showing Chong walking with his grandfather and playing happily with a troop of improbably large and somewhat humanized monkeys. The enemy are simply "many bad men" (8) who attack without warning. They force him and his family to hide in the jungle and make a journey of twenty-two days by foot to the Mekong River, his grandparents dying enroute. One of Ya Lee's illustrations shows Chong and his remaining family swimming across the river using small bamboo floats, the angle of the picture tilted to maximize the sense of danger and difficulty. Another illustration of an attacking soldier who haunts Chong's nightmares is replete with submachine gun, bandoleers of ammunition crossed on his chest, but is so vague as to make any attempt at identification by race or nationality impossible (9). Only the Thai border guards who steal the last of Chong's family's belongings at gunpoint have any specificity (13). In some ways, however, Chong is lucky since it has been reported that Hmong boys as young as twelve were recruited for battle (Goldfarb, 7). When Hiên, the Vietnamese child-protagonist of Tran-Khanh-Tuyet's *The Little Weaver of Thai-Yen Village*, is sent to her Aunt An's nearby village with a gift of rice, it is because their storehouse has been bombed, but no mention is made of who did the bombing. Although Hiên's father has been away fighting for eight years, it isn't clear, except by implication, that he's on what American children would be expected to consider the wrong side of the conflict.

The Vietnamese, Hmong and Cambodian characters involved in these stories do love their countries, but there is, in fact, little sense of what Westerners would call patriotism or political involvement in any of the books under consideration. The love they express is for the countryside itself, the trees, the mountains, the villages, their immediate families, neighbors and way of life. People are fighting, and people are dying, but the "why" of it simply is not relevant to either the child protagonists or their immediate guardians. The characters involved live their lives, trying to stay out of the way of the fighting, and flee when they have to. Whether or not this is actually the way people felt in the real world, whether or not one can even generalize from place to place and time to time about the motives of people of such diverse ethnic backgrounds, is unclear. After all, a number of the fathers absent from the stories did choose to go to war and not all of them, presumably, were drafted. But their reasons simply don't show up in these books for younger children. Only in *The Little Weaver of Thai-Yen Village* does the child protagonist show any real awareness that it is the Americans who have bombed her people. Soon after she is injured in the bombing raid, a "foreign woman" comes to her bedside and offers her the chance to have a "special operation" in the United States. Hiên is frightened by this idea at first; she "stared at the woman. She had kind eyes, but .... `wasn't it these foreigners who killed my mother and grandmother and bombed our villages?'" Still, realizing that if she doesn't accept the offer she may well die, "'I must survive if I want to help my people,' she thought. Turning toward the foreign woman, she nodded her head in agreement" (16). In the United States, although Hiên is lonely for the family and land she has lost, she accepts Mr. and Mrs. Wells, her new foster parents, with relatively little difficulty. It should be noted, however, that the specific political and military details do receive somewhat more attention in such novels for older children as Minfong Ho's *The Clay Marble* (1991), Linda Crew's *Children of the River* (1989), Sherry Garland's *Song of the Buffalo Boy (1992)* among others.

The specific details of how people get to the United States after the war differ to some extent, but are rarely dwelt upon at any length. Some children, like Anh in Mary Z. Holmes's *Dust of Life* and Hiên in *The Little Weaver* go through the *relatively* untraumatic experience of an airlift. Others, like the characters in *The Lotus Seed, Sweet Dried Apples*, or Michele Maria Surat's *Angel*, are boat people, forced to make terrifying sea voyages to achieve freedom. In *The Lotus Seed*, for example, Garland writes that "One terrible day her family scrambled into a crowded boat and set out on a stormy sea" (np) and Tatsuro Kiuchi's dark, double-page illustration for that text is violently unbalanced, depicting a small boat tipped sideways on a wave as heavy black clouds lour overhead. Ray's illustration of the fishing boat used in *Sweet Dried Apples* is less dramatic, but shows the boat sitting very low in the water and people sitting or standing quite literally on every square foot of deck or roof space available. Still other refugees, like Chong in *A Boy Named Chong*, Dia in *Dia's Story Cloth*, Little Mai in Pegi Dietz Shea's *The Whispering Cloth*, Nary in Margy Burns Knight's *Who Belongs Here? An American Story*, and the Prek family in Nancy Price Graff's *Where the River Runs* must undertake harrowing cross-country journeys through jungles and often across the Mekong river to reach the relative safety of the grossly overcrowded Thai refugee camps. Those Hmong families who reached Thailand were sometimes, depending on whim and the politics of the moment, not simply robbed by the Thai border guards, but turned back to Laos, beaten, or even raped. It has been estimated that as many as half the Hmong who set out on these treks perished in the attempt (Goldfarb, 10). Describing the Cambodian version of one such journey, Knight writes that

> Nary was sad and confused after his parents died. He cried as his grandmother carried him on her back through the jungle to Thailand. He had tried to run, but the blisters on his feet were bleeding. His uncle told him to be quiet because they were running from the soldiers and didn't want to be caught (np).

Only after spending years in mind-numbing poverty and boredom do Chong, Nary, Dia and their broken families gain permission to emigrate to the United States.

The novels for older children, for example Maureen Crane Wartski's *A Boat to Nowhere* (1980) or, more recently, Gloria Whelan's *Goodbye, Vietnam* (1992), devote much more space to these journeys than do the picture books for obvious reasons. One of the most basic books to describe the actual flight of Southeast Asian refugees from their homes in any detail is Sarah S. Kilborne's beginning chapter book *Leaving Vietnam, The True Story of Tuan Ngo* (1999). Using a boy named Tuan as her narrator, Kilborne shows the desperation of villagers fleeing a repressive post-war Vietnamese government. They must travel light, but must carry enough money and supplies with them to pay their passage and survive. They cannot afford to bring the whole family, and must leave Tuan's mother and younger brothers behind, hoping to make enough money in America to send for them later. They don't want to leave anyone who is ready to go, but too many people will sink the boat that awaits them. If they're caught they'll be put in a labor camp for five years. After a night's journey through the jungle, Tuan and his father reach the sea where a fishing boat awaits them. Crowding aboard, they speed away just ahead of the harbor guards who fire upon them. On the third day their engine dies and on the fourth day they run out of food. After five days at sea the people are thirsty, sunburned and desperate. Some

44

begin to go crazy and one old man jumps into the sea, only to be pulled back aboard. Pirates attack and steal all of the money and jewelry on board, although they also give the refugees water and fix their engine. Later, when a German tanker approaches, the refugees intentionally sink their own boat in order to force the other ship to pick them up; eventually it drops them off on an island which contains a refugee camp. After months of bureaucratic procedures, camp transfers, and waiting, Tuan and his father do eventually reach the United States. The year is 1983 and Tuan is eleven. The rest of his family reach America three years later.

Needless to say, despite the considerable detail and a number of frightening events, *Leaving Vietnam* is still a somewhat watered down account of the refugee experience. Not everyone who met with pirates found them this considerate. As Hoyt-Goldsmith briefly notes in *Hoang Anh*, "the most unfortunate people were those who met pirate ships. They were robbed, beaten, kidnapped, sold as slaves, or even tossed overboard. As a result many refugees have just disappeared completely" (8). Writing for an adult audience in *Strangers from a Different Shore*, Ronald Takaki can be even more explicit and recount a number of gruesome tales including that Luong Bot Chau: "The pirates chopped off one of her husband's fingers to get his ring and then tried to slit his throat. `But the knife they had was too blunt,' she said later. Instead they clubbed him to death and threw his body into the sea. Then they dragged the young girls up to the deck and systematically raped them" (453). And not everyone who threw himself into the sea like the old man in *Leaving Vietnam* was rescued. The percentage of boat people who died on their desperate journeys is unknown to this day. More realistic portrayals of the refugee experience written on a level that makes them accessible to younger children are found in Dia Cha's *Dia's Story Cloth, The Hmong People's Journey of Freedom* and Pegi Deitz Shea's *The Whispering Cloth, A Refugee Story*, both of which are illustrated with scenes from the Hmong *pa'ndau* or story cloth, Cha's book makes it clear that many people died. Cha's own father "was sent to fight in Xieng Khuang province. He never came back. We don't know whether he was killed or captured." Later we're told that "The communist soldiers shot at the Hmong men. The guerrilla soldiers came from their camps in the jungle and shot at the communists. Many people died" (np). In *The Whispering Cloth,* a portion of the *pa'ndau* scene is described thus: "Little Mai slept between her mother and father, who were very beautiful even though blood dripped from their heads. Grandmother put Mai in a basket on her back and ran through the paddies to the riverboats." (Shea, np). In one detail from the *pa'ndau* that illustrates Cha's book, we see an airplane dropping what is clearly labeled "Yellow Rain," on a Hmong village. Writing in *Multicultural Resources for Young Readers,* Daphne Muse identifies this as Agent Orange (453).

Ultimately, few of these books for younger children give a particularly detailed view of what war is like, but perhaps that's all for the good. As parents and teachers, regardless of our cultures of origin, we should want our children to understand where they, their friends, and their relatives came from and how their backgrounds have influenced them; but we also want to protect our children from the worst of the horrors the past has to offer. What is important is that, depending on the needs of the specific child, concerned parents and teachers do now have a variety of excellent books available, both fiction and non-fiction, on the various wars in Southeast Asia.

Chapter Four: A New World

Recently my family and I visited the Statue of Liberty and Ellis Island. The latter, of course, is now a museum dedicated to the history of immigration to the United States, both through the island itself and elsewhere. They have a computer on which you can look up your family name and see if anyone you're related to passed through their facilities. They also perform a series of plays about what it was like to land on Ellis Island as an immigrant in the late nineteenth and early twentieth centuries. There are dozens of displays of old photographs and old luggage, maps and charts. One display emphasizes the way immigration patterns have shifted over the years, with East and Southeast Asia, and Central America replacing Europe as major sources of new Americans. I found our visit to Ellis Island a moving experience.

My wife's people, many of them, go back to the Pilgrims; she's a direct descendent of Elder Brewster and even has a set of glasses, bought by her mother, which feature the logo of the Mayflower Society. Most of my people came over much more recently, Russian Jews fleeing pogroms and shtetl life, German Jews fleeing the Nazis, some of them through Ellis Island itself. My daughter, on the other hand, eleven years old as I write this, was born in an orphanage in Seoul, Korea. Her port of entry was O'Hare Airport in Chicago in April 1988. When it comes to the topic of immigration, our backgrounds thus make for something of a study in contrasts. We all have one thing in common, however--refugees. My wife's ancestors were refugees, as were mine. My daughter, born into a society that, despite its many excellences, simply won't accept children born out of wedlock, was a refugee of a different sort. I sometimes wonder how so many people manage to forget this overwhelming fact of American life, that nearly all of us are, or are the descendents of, refugees.

In this chapter we will concentrate on picture books about refugees from Southeast Asia and we will quickly discover that a number of themes appear over and over again: the need to adjust to a strange culture, one that makes assumptions about proper behavior that are violently at odds with what you are used to; the difficulty of dealing with various forms of post-traumatic stress disorder and depression; the often bitter sweet nostalgia for a home to which you can never return. Obviously each of the children and adults whose stories are told in the books we are looking at went through a slightly different refugee experience, the details will vary, but these themes will appear again and again in virtually all of the refugee narratives, both fiction and non-fiction, that we will be examining.

Another notable feature of these books is the lack of complete families and especially the absence of male relatives. The fathers of the children in *Sweet Dried Apples, The Lotus Seed, The Little Weaver of Thai-Yen Village,* and *Dia's Story Cloth* have all gone off to war, never to return. Chong's father isn't even mentioned in *A Boy Named Chong,* nor is Dara's in Sothea Chiemruom's *Dara's Cambodian New Year,* so we don't know what happened to them. Little Mai, in *The Whispering Cloth,* lost both of her parents in the war, as did Lan in *Dust of Life,* Lin in Lawrence McKay, Jr.'s *Journey Home,* and Nary in Margy Burns Knight's *Who Belongs Here?* Most of the children live with their mothers or, having lost both parents, with one or more grandparents or, in the case of *The Little Weaver,* American foster parents. Even those children, who have not lost a parent to the war itself, still tend to live in broken homes. Ut and her sisters in *Angel Child, Dragon Child,* and Huy in Kim-Lan Tran's *Têt: The New Year,* live with their fathers and mourn the fact that their families cannot yet afford to bring their mothers over from Vietnam. The Cambodian parents of Nancy Price Graff's *Where the River Runs* are both still alive, but have divorced and in *Journey Home* Mai's mother was abandoned by the father of her child before Mai was even born. Complete families, such as Anh's in *Dust of Life*, Dan Thuy's in Karen O'Connor's *Dan Thuy's New Life in America* or even the blended Saechao family of *A Mien Family* are clearly and tragically the exception. In his *Fighters, Refugees, Immigrants,* Goldfarb brings up the rarely mentioned fact that polygamy was a common practice in traditional Hmong families. When a Hmong man wanted to immigrate the United States, however, he was only allowed to bring one wife. This rule, apparently enforced by our government, led directly to the breakup of many families (36).

Americans, like most people I expect, prefer stories, even war stories, and particularly true ones, to involve a certain amount of hearty humor and to end with some equivalent of "and, reunited, they lived happily ever after." Unfortunately, in real life, such is rarely the case. In his recent book *John Wayne's America* the noted historian Garry Wills, following the lead of Eric Bentley, suggests that the sanitized and highly romantic war movies popularized by John Wayne and others in the 1940s, 50s, and 60s made it relatively easy for Americans to send their children to Korea and Vietnam (12-14). It was only after the war got going, the body bags began coming home, and those veterans who returned from their tours of duty began to show symptoms of depression and what we now call post-traumatic stress disorder, that Americans really began to recognize something that veterans of earlier wars could have told them all along. The horror and pain of war doesn't stop when the guns cease firing. As marine veteran Michael Norman wrote:

> Family and friends wondered why we were so angry. What are you crying about? They would ask. Why are you so ill-tempered and disaffected. Our fathers and grandfathers had gone off to war, done their duty, come home and got on with it. What made our generation so different? As it turns out, nothing. No difference at all. When old soldiers from "good" wars are dragged from behind the curtain of myth and sentiment and brought into the light, they too seem to smolder with choler and alienation.... We were angry as all civilized men who have ever been sent to make murder in the name of virtue were angry. (Herman, quoting Norman, 27)

And it wasn't very different for the civilians caught up in the war either. Samphy Iep, who works for the International Rescue Committee and who had lived in the United States for a decade, was interviewed by John Tenhula for his book *Voices from Southeast Asia*:

> *Do you still see yourself as a refugee?*
> Oh, that's a very difficult question....Well, yes, I do. I am a United States citizen now, but psychologically I still feel homeless. I dream in Khmer and talk in English. That's the conflict. It won't go away. That is my difference between East and West. I dream of the Khmer Rouge, killings and murder. I talk in a different language—English—about life in the suburbs of Washington, D.C. It is quite a contrast, isn't it? (Tenhula, 30)

Whether it's called "shell shock" or "battle fatigue" or depression, or nightmares, or PTSD, the trauma of war can continue to effect survivors for years, even decades, after the war is over, and not just adults. Children, unfortunately, are equally vulnerable to such trauma.

One of the things clearly shared by many of the child characters (and the adults for that matter) in the books being considered here is some form of prolonged depression or post-traumatic stress disorder; their symptoms include nightmares, repressed memories, an inability to speak of the past, and flashback memories of near hallucinogenic power. In *A Boy Named Chong*, the young Hmong protagonist recounts how, after being forced to run from his village, "When I slept I had nightmares for over one year" (8). Nam-Huong, the Vietnamese protagonist of Diana Kidd's beginning chapter book *Onion Tears*, suffers from intense flashbacks. Having reached Australia in a small, overcrowded boat, she finds herself unable to tell others about what she has experienced and she suffers from a horrible fear of the ocean. One day while playing, Nam-Huong climbs a tree and this triggers a memory of her lost younger sister, Lan. Then, looking out over the ocean from the top of the tree, it's like she's back on the boat that brought her to Australia:

> There was sea everywhere. Everywhere I looked.
> And where the sea ended and the sky began, I thought I saw a boat.
> . . . It was just a little boat with hundreds of people in it with scared eyes, and sad eyes, and eyes drowned in tears—and Grandpa and me. Grandpa was squashed up close to me and he held my hand and put his arm around me when the waves leaped at us across the deck like snarling tigers. . .

50

Every day there was less and less rice for us to eat. But Grandpa always said he wasn't hungry, and he made me eat his share of rice—his little handful.

And when there was no rice or water left, Grandpa and I clung tightly to each other—and we drifted and dreamed through suns as orange as saffron and nights that wrapped around us like black monsters.

Our little boat floated for days and weeks like a leaf on the edge of the world, and I dreamed of a wave as high as a mountain. . . .

But when, one day, I opened my eyes, there was only the sea screaming around us.

And Grandpa's hand was limp in mine (51-52).

Later, while playing with a dog, Nam-Huong chases him through some bushes and:

Suddenly the bushes ended and there was the wild, screaming sea.

And for a moment I was on the boat again and the water was gold around the silent bodies I saw floating there—floating on the saffron sea, staring at the saffron sun—and I saw my Grandpa there, silently floating away.

"ONG NOI! ONG NOI!" I screamed. "GRANDPA! GRANDPA!" (54).

Eventually Nam-Huong is able to pour out her heart to a sympathetic adult: "Miss Lily sat and listened while I told her everything. I told her about my mom and dad. And then I told her about Grandpa. I told her about the boat. I told Miss Lily everything" (55).

Huy, the young protagonist of *Têt: The New Year*, feels only sadness when he thinks of the upcoming Vietnamese holiday. His father, "so lonely and so lost in the new country," (5) apparently spends most of his time depressed. "My father says we don't celebrate Têt here. He says, `No country--no New Year.'" Dara's grandfather in *Dara's Cambodian New Year* appears to be similarly depressed; he just "sits in his room and feels sad" (2). In *Where the River Runs*, the author explains that the boy

Buttra, his mother and grandmother, and many of the other Cambodian refugees in this country have terrifying nightmares about the `sour and bitter time' and the years they spent in refugee camps. By day, they carry with them everywhere a burden of sorrow. It is like a heavy suitcase they would like to put down but cannot, full of anger and tears shed over the loss of their families and the destruction of their country. (52)

Perhaps the most explicit depiction of depression and post-traumatic stress disorder, however, is found in Mary Z. Holmes's portrait of the refugee child Lan in the beginning chapter book *Dust of Life*.

Lan's parents are both dead and she's been in a refugee camp but, when she finally reaches America in 1980, she, like Nam Huong of *Onion Tears*, won't tell her remaining family many of the details. She seems to fit into American society at first and appears happy, however this happiness proves to be incredibly brittle. When Lan learns that Mt. St. Helens has blown up, she finds it traumatic even though the mountain is hundreds of miles away, because the event destroys her fragile belief in the stability of the United States. Lan becomes depressed, refusing to go to work or even leave the house. Anh, the narrator of *Dust of Life* says that:

> When I invited her to come and watch my skating lesson, she said no. It was difficult to get her outside even to the garden. Something was terribly wrong. Whenever I asked, Lan told me she was very happy, everything was okay. But she was being polite. Day by day, Lan wilted more and talked less. Even the thought of Ut coming to dinner on Sunday didn't cheer her up. (28)

The young woman Ut comments that such depression is common among refugees who had a hard time in Vietnam (29). Only after Lan is able, again like Nam-Huong in *Onion Tears,* to tell her story do we realize the true horror of what she's lived through and the extent to which she's internalized feelings of worthlessness and inferiority (36). Interestingly enough, Anh, Lan's much less traumatized and painstakingly American cousin, who'd reached the United States via the airlift some five years earlier, eventually realizes that she too has unconsciously shared these feelings. Finally able to gain some perspective on her problem, Lan decides that she wants to go to college and "become a woman who helps other Vietnamese women.... Help with troubles in heart....Help with troubles in mind." (42). Lan wants to become a psychologist. Such difficulties are equally common in the Vietnamese-American, Cambodian-American, and Hmong-American communities. Problems with depression are so serious in the Hmong community, in fact, particularly among elders, that physicians have actually begun discussing what they call "Hmong sudden-death syndrome, an affliction that has taken the lives of more than 100 former soldiers between the ages 30-50. Family members speculate that the cause is intense grief" (*Hmong in America* 81, paraphrasing Takaki, 465). In this context it is worth noting that in many cases the Hmong, Vietnamese, and Cambodian survivors of the various wars in Southeast Asia, including the children, have often been through experiences much worse than those actually recorded in most English-language texts, and especially children's books. In *Kou Chang's Story: The Journey of a Laotian Hmong Refugee Family*, for example, a young Hmong man, describes how

> Many families had many children and they couldn't find food for all the children. So they threw their children away before the children had even died. Some people couldn't throw their children away because the children were still alive, so they gave a lot of opium and herbs to the children to eat, so that the children died....Some parents died but the children were still alive. Nobody took care of the children and they eventually died, too. Some mothers were killed but the babies didn't know that their mothers had died and they still sucked the breast of their mothers because they thought their mothers slept (Chang, 190).

This is indeed the stuff of nightmare.

As has been widely discussed in recent years by therapists such as Lenore Terr in *Too Scared to Cry,* the best cure for post-traumatic stress disorder, and indeed for many forms of depression, is simply talking about the trauma (302). Sandra J. Lindow has suggested, applying Terr's theories to the children's books of Ursula K. Le Guin, that "Trauma cannot be healed in isolation; the act of creating the traumatic narrative and sharing it with others begins to defuse the overwhelming emotions that have frozen intact and continue to threaten the survivor through anxiety attacks, nightmares, and flashbacks" (37). In *Dust of Life* Lan gains perspective on her trauma and starts on the road to recovery only after she gives a detailed account of those traumatic events, first to her cousin Anh, and then to the rest of the family, and learns in the process that she will not be rejected. Doing this is not easy. There seems to be an innate unwillingness to discuss such events. Nam-Huong in *Onion Tears,* who clearly suffers from post-traumatic stress disorder, can not tell her story to anyone at first. Only after finally doing so, nearly a year after coming to Australia, can she both cry for her dead and get on with her life. Actually, you don't even have to be a full-fledged refugee to go through this experience. The novelist Minfong Ho was never a refugee herself, but suffered from PTSD after working at a refugee camp on the Thai-Cambodian border. In her essay "The Shaping of *The Clay Marble*" she reveals that "It was very difficult to talk about Cambodia, about the Cambodian refugees. Without my having acknowledged it, I had been sucked into the conspiracy of silence that is so often generated by absolute misery. The Cambodian refugees themselves had not spoken much of their own suffering. How could I? One does not talk about such unspeakable things" (142).

Similarly, in book after book Southeast Asian refugees, after suffering for a time in silence, do try to come to terms with the sadness of what they've lost by remembering the past, by discussing it with others, by carrying out important rituals from the old country, by adapting to their new nation, and, ultimately, by contemplating a return to their homeland. In Tran's *Têt: The New Year*, for example, a boy's father is able to escape depression only after he is convinced to share with other refugees in a celebration of this most important of Vietnamese holidays. In Chiemruom's *Dara's Cambodian New Year,* Dara rescues his grandfather from depression by painting him scenes from the old country about which they then reminisce. The traditional celebration of the New Year is clearly of enormous symbolic importance in both books: an affirmation of the old ways, combined with a looking forward to the new. This is also obviously the case in Xiong's *The Gift, The Hmong New Year,* in which a young girl shares her cultural traditions with her classmates and thereby gains an increased sense of self-worth. Indeed, as Lenore Terr has suggested, for many children school and education itself can be a partial cure for the depression and poor sense of self-worth so common to refugee children. She reports on a study in which fifty children who had recently immigrated from Cambodia were rated on

> school grades and school comportment. Both were consistently good. These Cambodian kids were remarkably industrious students, no matter how repeatedly traumatized or how depressed they were. Many had been cutoff

from school for years while they were incarcerated in the Pol Pot regime's concentration camps. Once they reached America, however, they bounced right back at school. The healthiest part of these youngsters' lives was school. (193).

In Garland's *The Lotus Seed* an elderly woman has saved a seed from the last Vietnamese emperor's garden as a keepsake, and mourns terribly when it is misplaced by one of her grandchildren. Later, however, the lost seed takes root in American soil and a new lotus blossoms, providing both the old woman and her grandchildren with something concrete to help them remember the past. The young narrator, having received a seed from the new plant, says that she wrapped it " in a piece of silk and hid it in a secret place. Someday I will plant it and give the seeds to my own children and tell them about the day my grandmother saw the emperor cry" (np). The value of keepsakes, physical objects from the old country, is something that comes up again and again. Her lotus seed from the Emperor's garden is enormously precious to the grandmother. When it is found newly sprouting in the garden, she proclaims that it is "the flower of life and hope....No matter how ugly the mud or how long the seed lies dormant, the bloom will be beautiful. It is my country" (np). When the title character of *Hoang Breaks the Lucky Teapot*, accidentally smashes his *gia truyen*, the family's greatest treasure, which had been given to him by his grandmother "on the scary night when they left their home in Vietnam" (np), he feels like the family will have nothing but bad fortune unless he can repair or replace the heirloom. In *Journey Home*, Lin, a Vietnamese war orphan grown to adulthood in the United States, has only a shabby paper kite to connect her to her place of birth, but as if by magic, it becomes the key that allows her to solve the riddle of her past. Finally, in *The Whispering Cloth*, Little Mai, her parents dead, lives in a refugee camp on the Thai border with her grandmother, her life centered on the creation of *pa'ndau*, the traditional Hmong story cloths. At first Mai is only allowed to sew borders and details on cloths created by others, but she longs to make a *pa'ndau* of her own to sell for money to fly to America. Eventually Mai receives permission to create her own *pa'ndau*, but is unable to come up with a subject. Then, one night, when she is crying for her dead parents,

Mai's grandmother says to her "Call to them, Mai. Call their spirits with the words in your fingers" (np) and the little girl immediately finds her subject, her own life story. Although her original intent was to sell the *pa'ndau,* Mai eventually decides that the cloth, which represents her life and her people's history, is too precious to part with.

> Mai picked up the *pa'ndau,* but the wind blew it back against her. The short, rough stitches of her father's hand stood up from the cloth to stroke Mai's chin. She tried to speak, but the smooth stitches of her mother's cheeks hushed her lips.
> "Mai?" Grandma nudged her. "How much?"
> "Nothing," Mai whispered, clutching the story cloth.
> "Nothing?"
> "The *pa'ndau* tells me it is not for sale." (np)

As Dia Cha says in her book *Dia's Story Cloth,* "it is important for me to remember everything the Hmong have been through....When I show the story cloth to my niece and nephew, who were born here in the United States, I point to different pictures and tell them that this is what it was like" (np). Remembering the past is vital, but sharing those memories is equally important. In each of the books mentioned above, characters must do both to overcome their sadness and regain their mental health.

Chapter Five: Memories and the Return Home

Over the years the United States has been continuously revitalized by those who come to us as refugees and by the customs those refugees bring with them. Few newcomers to our country have had any desire to make a complete break with their past, and especially not those who left their homelands unwillingly or to escape persecution. In Chapter Four we discussed the importance of memory, it's value as a means of healing the scars that so often are part of each refugee's inheritance. Much as mourners at a funeral come to terms with their recent loss by remembering and speaking fondly (or sometimes profanely) of the deceased, those who have lost their country of origin often need to speak of both their homeland and their ordeal before their healing can be complete, or, in some cases, even begin. This was made explicit in chapter books aimed at somewhat older children, like *Onion Tears* and *Dust of Life*, but was also clear on a more implicit level in *A Boy Named Chong, The Whispering Cloth, The Lotus Seed*, and other picture books.

One aspect of this remembering is a deep-seated longing to return to the land the refugee has lost. Those who came to the United States as adults may well never feel at home in our country, may well never come to terms with their loss. In *Fighters, Refugees, Immigrants* Goldfarb reports that many Hmong men, their primary skills as farmers and soldiers no longer needed, have had great difficulty adjusting to the United States and, years after coming to this country, still "talk of going back to their homeland to fight against the government in Laos" (36). In picture books such as *Dara's Cambodian New Year*, *The Lotus Seed*, and *Têt: The New Year* we met grownups who were clearly having enormous trouble making the adjustment, grownups who, suffering from what may well be clinical depression, would give anything to return to their homelands if it were possible to do so. In each of these books, however, the author chose to end on an optimistic note, with the parent or grandparent making at least a partial adjustment to his or her new world in the book's final pages, often with the help of a child. Remembering Ronald Takaki's grim statistics on Hmong Sudden Death Syndrome (465-66), as mentioned in Chapter Four, of course, we know that such is not always the case. This preference for optimistic endings, although not without some truth, can thus be seen, I think, as being as much the authors' response to the needs of their child-readers for a final affirmative statement about their elders as it is a reflection of reality.

Their parents, grandparents and other adult caretakers are invariably of great importance to the children in the books we've been examining. Indeed, one of the strongest recurring themes in these stories is the importance of family. Nonetheless with a very few exceptions, the adults we've encountered are generally secondary figures. Children, after all, although dependent on their adult caretakers, are generally most interested in other children and their concerns. At the center of many of these books, therefore, are the attitudes of young people toward the old country. Sometimes, as in *The Dust of Life* or *Dan Thuy's New Life in America*, the children are old enough to remember their homelands. Sometimes, as in Sherry Garland's *My Father's Boat*, Jeremy Schmidt and Ted Wood's *Two Lands, One Heart* (subtitled *An American Boy's Journey to His Mother's Vietnam*), Diane Hoyt-Goldsmith's *Hoang Anh, A Vietnamese-American Boy*, Felice Blanc's *I Am Vietnamese American* or Lawrence McKay, Jr.'s *Journey Home*, the children either were too young when they left Southeast Asia to have any memory of the country of their birth, or, alternately, they were born in the United States, or in some cases a Thai or Taiwanese relocation camp, and have never even seen their homelands.

One connection between adults and children that holds true in virtually all of these stories, once again, is the adults' desire that their children learn and remember as much as is possible about their traditions, their language, and their homelands. For example, the grandfathers in *Dara's Cambodian New Year* and *The Gift* take great pleasure in teaching their grandchildren about the world they've lost. Dat, the five year old narrator of Linda Smith's *Dat's New Year,* is fortunate enough to have both a father and a mother to teach him what he needs to know. In *Hoang Anh, A Vietnamese-American Boy,* the book's child narrator considers it a great honor when he gets to meet and talk with Phuc Huu Tran a noted Vietnamese scholar visiting in the United States. Finally, Xiong, the oldest boy in the Vang family in *A Hmong Family,* is quite clear on the importance of learning about his culture:

> ....As the oldest son in my family, I know that someday I'll have to keep many of the Hmong customs alive for my parents and for my children.
> Even though I'll be an American citizen soon, I'll want my own son to speak the Hmong language and take care of me when I take my journey to heaven someday too. I know my son will be happy here in America, too (61).

As Xiong's father says, "Our goal is to raise our children to be leaders for the next generations of Hmong here in America....But we also believe that our children should never forget where they've come from and what it means to be Hmong" (55).

Sometimes, however, simply remembering the old country isn't enough, especially when friends and relatives were left behind. A possible final step in the healing process is the return home. Many of the characters in these books, both real and fictional, speak longingly of their desire to return to their native lands or, in the case of those children born in the United States or in camps, to see their parents' birthplace. In *The Little Weaver of Thai-Yen Village*, written in the late 1970's, Hien "did not know if she would ever return to her village again, but she vowed never to forget her country or her people"(22). The narrator of the more recent *Sweet Dried Apples*, however, closes his story by saying "Someday, I promised myself, I will find a way back" (np). Tran in Blanc's *I Am Vietnamese American* has put a map of Vietnam that his grandmother gave him up on his bedroom wall next to his map of the United States. He says that his grandmother has promised him that "someday we'll visit the country my family came from. My dad says that we'll also take a trip across America, to learn more about the country we live in" (22). Dan Tram, the sister of the title character in O'Connor's *Dan Thuy's New Life in America,* has become increasingly Americanized, but feels a pull in both directions. O'Connor quotes her as saying "When I lived in Vietnam, I wished I lived in the United States. But when I came here I wished I could go back to Vietnam to see my friends and my other grandparents" (32). Similarly of two minds is Debbie, a Cambodian girl now living in the United States. Interviewed by Stephanie St. Pierre in her *Teenage Refugees from Cambodia Speak Out,* she says

> Someday I'd like to go back to Cambodia. I'm the youngest child in the family, the fifth one. My mom and older brother came over here. My older sisters, two of them and a brother, all died. It was while we were trying to escape, because of hunger, I think. I was so young I guess it didn't really affect me. I was only four months old when we left. I never knew what my dad looked like. I imagine if I went back to Cambodia I wouldn't know how things work over there. I'm just so used to everything here (45-46).

Sherry Garland's recent *My Father's Boat,* concerns a Vietnamese-American fisherman who speaks with sorrow of the father he hasn't seen in twenty years and then vows to his own son "Someday I will go back and take you to meet your grandfather. I will show you his beautiful boat, and together we will cast our nets into the South China Sea" (np). The boy is filled with longing to meet his grandfather and wonders

> If my grandfather's hands are strong and callused, too. Or if he sings to the dolphins the way my father does. I wonder if he thinks of us while he sips his steaming tea or while he casts his nets over the water (np).

Asked by his son if he misses his own father, the fisherman replies: "Yes.... More than the mountains and rivers more than the waving fields of rice" (np). Bringing their catch to shore, the father and son head for their Gulf Coast home. As the boy falls asleep he dreams "that we are together—my grandfather, my father, and I—out on the lonely sea in my father's beautiful boat" (np).

In recent years relations between the United States and Vietnam have slowly improved. Indeed, two days ago as I write our local newspaper carried an AP story headlined "U.S., Vietnam reach agreement on trade," and described the event as "the last step in normalizing relations" between the two countries (*Leader Telegram*, 4A).

It has therefore now become possible for at least some of the refugees who came to the United States from Southeast Asia to return to their homes, if only for a visit. To my knowledge no children's book has yet been published about people choosing to leave the United States and return home to Vietnam, Cambodia, or Laos on a permanent basis, but two recent children's books do portray Vietnamese-American children's short-term visits to Vietnam and their meetings with long-lost relatives. The first, the beautifully photographed chapter book *Two Lands, One Heart*, is written on a fifth grade level and begins with an introduction which briefly describes the fate of three Vietnamese children in 1975. Their parents missing and presumed dead, they fled through great danger to an orphanage in Saigon. Eventually they wound up in America where, unlike many Vietnamese brothers and sisters, they were fortunate enough to all be adopted into the same American family. In 1990, Phit, now named Heather, the oldest of the children, married and with children of her own, flew back to Vietnam in search of her lost family. Despite a lack of immediate success she refused to give up hope and, a year later, she discovered that her parents were still alive. She and her husband immediately returned to Vietnam for a reunion. Then, in 1994, accompanied by her adoptive mother and aunt, she again visited her homeland, bringing with her half-Vietnamese, American-born oldest son, Timothy James, or TJ, age seven. The bulk of the book is the story of TJ's visit. Although the briefly told tale of Phit's childhood is heartbreaking enough, TJ's story is almost entirely upbeat, an account of what it's like to take a really swell overseas trip by air to an exotic and beautiful country. TJ meets a variety of doting relatives, discovers any number of interesting customs and foods, gets to ride in bicycle taxis and on oxen, spends time on the water and generally has a wonderful vacation. Among other places he visits, however, is a section of Vietnam War-era tunnels outside of Saigon which have been rehabilitated as a historic monument. Although he at first sees the tunnels as a delightful playground, a guide explains their grim history and eventually

> TJ decides there is nothing fun about the tunnels. These dark, cramped dens are the only place in Vietnam where he will see evidence of the war that tore this country apart and sent his mother to America (17).

The second story, *Journey Home*, a picture book written on a third/fourth grade level, contains several parallels to Phit's story in the introduction to *Two Lands, One Heart*. It concerns a ten year-old, half-Vietnamese-American girl's trip to her mother's homeland in search of lost roots. Lin, Mai's mother, was a war orphan who, after coming to the United States and being adopted by Americans, grew up to have a successful career as a research scientist. She knows even less about her parents or her own background than did TJ's mom in *Two Lands, One Heart*. The only clues to her identity are a kite, Lin's one possession when she came to America, and a photograph of her holding the kite as a small child at the Vietnamese orphanage. Adding poignancy to the search, for Mai at least, is the fact that her own father, a man named Frank Mercer, evidently abandoned her mother before Mai was born.

Lin and Mai prepare for their trip by reading as much as they can on Vietnam, Buddhism, and Kuan Yin, the Vietnamese Goddess of Mercy. Traditionally, we're told, it is believed that "At the cry of misery, Kuan Yin hears the voice, then removes the sorrow" (np). Arriving in Saigon, now known as Ho Chi Minh City, Mai and her mother first visit the People's Hall of Records but fail to discover anything significant. They then try the city's many orphanages without success. Feeling depressed, Lin and Mai go for a walk through a marketplace and, to their surprise, come across a street merchant who is selling kites similar to the one in the photograph. This eventually sends them on a trip into the countryside and leads them to Tran Quang Tai, an old friend of Lin's father. Many years ago, Lin and Mai discover, Tran had placed Lin in the orphanage because her parents had died in the war and his own life was too precarious to allow him to keep her. The kite she'd brought with her to America was her father's handiwork, left with her by Tran. Learning of her parents' fate, seeing where she was born, and hearing for the first time her real name, Lin begins to cry,

62

something her daughter Mai has never seen her do before. Her tears, however, signify closure. Although, unlike Phit in *Two Lands, One Heart*, she will never be reunited with her parents, Lin has finally found the answers to her life-long questions. When her daughter asks "is this home?" Lin replies

> Inside me, yes, because here I was born. But the world changes, Mai, and even though I lived through the change, I have been away too long....I've found what I thought I'd never find, my name, and for that I'll never again feel the emptiness of not knowing. That can never be taken away from me (np).

For seven year-old TJ Vietnam is a wonderful place to visit, but it isn't home. At the end of *Two Lands, One Heart* he's sorry to be leaving his new-found relatives, but he misses his dad and his brothers. For Mai, though, three years older than TJ and far more aware of her mother's pain (not to mention her own lack of a father), things are a bit more complex. Earlier, in Ho Chi Minh City, she'd felt the strangeness of being, for the first time in her life, in a place where pretty much everyone looked like her, a place where in a certain way she belonged as she has never belonged before. Now, though, their quest has come to a conclusion. Her mother finally knows the truth about her parents and her past while Mai has discovered in herself a new sense of maturity, a new feeling of being centered in the world.

> Where is home, I wonder. Is it inside me, like Mom says, or all around me? I was born in America and my name is Mai. Yet when I look into Tran Quang Tai's eyes, I feel like I belong here, too. I think home must be inside me and all around me too (np).

Some immigrants, whether they come from Southeast Asia or Central America or the old Soviet Block, become almost totally acclimatized to their new homes. Others remain outsiders their entire lives. For most, however, it's a partial process. As the years go by they gradually fit in to their new societies with greater and greater ease. They may even cease for a time to feel like outsiders. Then, however, something will happen. A snatch of music, an old acquaintance, a picture in a book, the smell of a traditional food, will remind them that where they're currently living can never truly be their home. The desire to go back may always be present, impractical, perhaps, in many cases, but impossible to completely overcome. Talk to someone from Vietnam or Laos (or anywhere in Asia for that matter) and you will invariably discover that one of the most unpleasant aspects of their lives in the United States is their occasional encounters with racism. No matter how successful or acclimatized they may be, no matter how well they dress or speak English, on one day or another they are sure to have run into a white (or occasionally black) American, usually a young male, himself, ironically enough, the descendent of immigrants, who will taunt them, shouting at them to go home, to go back where they came from. I wonder how many would, if it were possible?

Chapter Six: Dealing with Racism

Although the Vietnam War is now a quarter of a century behind us, its origins and the role the United States played in it are still controversial, matters of strongly conflicting ideology. It can even be argued that a significant part of the virulent, seemingly irrational hatred many conservatives in this country feel for President Clinton can be traced directly to his youthful and rather mild anti-war activities. Equally controversial, perhaps, is our nation's ongoing attempt to come to terms with racism and the role of minorities in American public life. Our nation has not done a particularly good job of assimilating its rapidly growing Southeast Asian immigrant population and, as a result, has seen an increase in both racially motivated violence against Southeast Asians and, in what may be a natural defense mechanism, the development of Vietnamese, Hmong and Cambodian youth gangs. In this chapter I will consider the extent to which the children's books under consideration here deal with the difficult issue of racism, either ideologically or in practical terms. I will also examine the extent to which these books can be used with children of other ethnic groups to help them understand the Southeast Asian experience.

Most of the books being discussed here attempt, to a greater or lesser extent, to speak to both a general audience and a specific Southeast Asian ethnic group. Most attempt to keep our interest and engage our sympathy by centering on a specific family or, in many cases, an individual child. Some of the books, like Graff's *Where the River Runs* and O'Connor's *Dan Thuy's New Life in America*, move back and forth between the immediate lives of the families being described and the general history of the relevant ethnic group. Others, like Garland's *The Lotus Seed,* Breckler's *Sweet Dried Apples* and the Marchants' *A Boy Named Chong,* stick very closely to a powerful and moving personal story. At least two of the books under consideration, however, are designed with the explicit intent of teaching ethnic and racial tolerance.

Michele Maria Surat's *Angel Child, Dragon Child* relates the story of Ut, one of five Vietnamese immigrant sisters who are attending school in the United States for the first time. On the first day of classes the girls wear their best Vietnamese-style clothes to school which, unfortunately, look like pajamas to their American classmates, who tease the sisters unmercifully. The illustrator, Vo-Dinh Mai makes a point of showing the girls' tormenters to be of a variety of different races. Although the majority of the children doing the teasing are European American, several African-American children are also involved, as well as one little girl who may well be Asian American (6-7). Raymond, a little white boy with firey red hair is particularly obnoxious, riding Ut on a regular basis over the weeks that follow. On the day of the first snowfall Raymond hits Chi Hai, Ut's sister, with a snowball and, when Ut responds in kind, he physically attacks her. As punishment the principal sends them to detention and orders them to work together to put Ut's story down on paper, with the girl dictating to Raymond. At first angry and unrepentent, Raymond continues to taunt Ut but, when he begins to cry for his mother, the Vietnamese girl comforts him. Eventually, she shares a cookie with him as well as the secret of her matchbox, in which she carries a picture of her mother who is still in Vietnam. On this small foundation, a friendship is built, and the assignment is completed. Later the principal reads the story to the entire school and Raymond suggests that the students hold a Vietnamese fair to raise enough money to bring Ut's mother to America.

Surat does a particularly good job of showing how the taunting Ut receives directly connects with her own feelings of insecurity. Just before entering the schoolyard for the first time Ut notes that, although her four sisters are skipping two by two ahead of her, there is no mother to skip with her or to tell her to "Be happy in your new American school" (4). To be met immediately after this sad thought by such extreme unpleasantness could indeed be devastating to a young girl. Ut's first reaction is to turn around and go home, but her older sister tells her that she can't. Just then the bell rings and everyone rushes into the building. In a panicky moment, Ut immediately loses track of her sisters and discovers herself surrounded by "a swirl of rushing children. `Pa-jaa-mas!' they teased " (7). Entering the school, she finds her classroom wildly different from what she's used to. Close to tears, she loses most of her English, which provokes even more taunting. Only the memory of her mother sustains her through the day. Weeks later, when Raymond hits her sister with the snowball, part of the anger in Ut's response is probably the result of the boy's bad timing. Ut has had very little to be happy about over the past few weeks in school and her discovery of snow is a rare occasion for joy:

> I whispered, "this is snow. It makes everything soft, even the angry trees with no leaves to make them pretty."
> My fingers danced on the desktop while I waited for the bell. When it rang, I rushed out the door.
> Outside, snowflakes left wet kisses on my cheeks. "Chi Hai!" I called. "Catch some!"
> "It disappears!" she cried.
> Just as Chi Hai spoke, a snowrock stung her chin. That red-haired boy darted behind the dumpster. He was laughing hard (14-16).

It's worth noting, however, that, despite the pain Raymond causes Ut and her sisters, his and the other children's attacks never become as bad as they might be. He has seized primarily on the girls' clothing, worn only on the first day of school, as the object of his ridicule and later, when told he must write Ut's story, says that he can't do it because he "can't understand her funny words" (18). There are, however, none of the specific references to eyes or skin color and none of the obscene names, so frequently used by racists. Raymond's prejudices are apparently simply against those who are different, rather than having any actual conscious grounding in racism per se. When he finally gets to know Ut as an individual, his prejudices are quickly overcome and, of course, he even helps set up a fundraiser to bring her mother to America. The message of *Angel Child, Dragon Child* is clear, if somewhat simplistic. For small children at least, prejudice is simply a matter of ignorance, something to be easily overcome through improved communication and increased knowledge.

More explicitly didactic and written for a somewhat older audience than Surat's picture book is Knight's *WhoBelongs Here? An American Story*. At the center of the book is Nary, a young Cambodian boy who lives in the United States with his grandmother and his uncle, having emigrated from a refugee camp in Thailand several years after his parents were murdered by the Pol Pot regime. *Who Belongs Here?* tells a fairly standard refugee's saga, giving a bit more detail than most of the other picture books on the hardships the boy has had to live through. In his American school Nary, like Ut and her sisters, runs into prejudice. The prejudice he meets differs from that which Ut encounters, however, in that it is specifically and clearly brought about by racism.

One day, while he is getting books out of his locker, Nary is accosted in the school hallway by two white classmates who insult him, saying "'Hey, chink, out of my way.' `Yeah, get back on the boat and go home where you belong'"(np). On another occasion, Nary is called a "gook" and told that he doesn't belong in the U.S. The boy speaks to his teacher about the problem, and the teacher sets up a social studies class activity in which the students are all required to pretend that they themselves are refugees who must convince a guard who does not speak English to give them asylum. Writing for somewhat older children, Knight avoids the perhaps oversimplied, "happily ever after" ending which is appropriate for the early-elementary school audience of *Angel Child, Dragon Child*. The end of *Who Belongs Here?* is not all sweetness and light, but we are told that.

> Nary is working hard to make the U.S. his new home. He likes to be with his friends and he is learning to play the drums. . . .He also hopes people in his new country can learn to get along (np).

This paragraph is accompanied by a picture of Nary, surrounded by other children of several different racial backgrounds, working on the school yearbook. While Knight emphasizes the fact that Nary must preserve his connection to the old ways of his

68

people—we're told that he's learning "to write Khmer so he can keep in touch with his relatives"(np)—she also wants to emphasize the importance of his connecting with children of other ethnic backgrounds.

Allan Baillie, speaking of his own Young Adult novel, *Little Brother*, but in a way that clearly illustrates another of Knight's purposes in *Who Belongs Here?*, says "why tell children about Cambodia? Because children like them suffered in Cambodia and maybe there is a Cambodian in the class. Look at that weird refugee kid, he might have gone through something like this. Maybe he's a bit nervous, doesn't talk much about his past, has trouble laughing. Understand him a little, give him some time" (152-53). Knight and Baillie clearly believe that it is absolutely vital that American children understand what refugees are and what they've gone through. Equally important, children must learn to avoid seeing refugees as "them," as *those* people who came to *our* country. Children, as demonstrated in the social studies activity that Nary's teacher carries out, must begin to see *themselves* as refugees or, at the very least, as their direct descendents. They must learn to see refugees not as *them* but, on some level at least, as *us*.

What makes *Who Belongs Here?* unusual, however, is the way in which Nary's story is interwoven not just with a brief history of the Cambodian refugees, but with American refugee and minority history in general. Italicized paragraphs, separate from the main narrative, explain how the United States has largely been built by refugees and various minority groups, and give specific details about Ellis Island, the on-going plight of Mexican-American migrant workers, the influence of the Iroquois nation on the U.S. Constitution, the great nineteenth-century wave of Irish immigration, and so forth. Short paragraphs mention specific heroes in immigrant history, for example, Dith Pran, who "escaped from the killing fields of Cambodia...[and now] travels around the U.S. talking about his hopes for his homeland" and Dolores Huerta, who "also travels around the U.S. giving talks... [and] help[ing] organize farm laborers" (np). Anne Sibley O'Brien's colorful pictures jump back and forth, sometimes illustrating Nary's story, sometimes the more heavily didactic historical text. Underlining the intent of the author that the book be used as a teaching text, Knight, along with Thomas V. Chan, has also published the *Who Belongs Here? Activity Guide*, which contains some thirty useful, student-oriented activities related to the book or to the topic of immigration in general. Among these activities are lessons in which children explore the origins of their names, make a list of what they'd take with them if they were to become refugees, learn about the many English words that come from various other cultures, and try to decide what standards should govern who is allowed to settle in the United States.

Children rarely understand racism, whether they are its victims or, imitating their elders, its perpetrators, but teaching children how not to be racist can be a difficult task even under the best of circumstances. Recently Benjamin Smith, a young man from Wilmette, Illinois, an upper-middle class suburb just north of Skokie, Illinois, the heavily Jewish middle class suburb where my parents live, went on a rampage across Illinois and Indiana, randomly murdering Ricky Byrdsong, the popular African-American former basketball coach at Northwestern University and a Korean college student, shooting several other members of minority groups, including a number of Asians and Orthodox Jews. Well known on his college campus for his racist beliefs and his membership in the violently racist and anti-semitic Peoria, Illinois-based Church of the Creator, Smith had previously been interviewed by a student reporter at Indiana University and, after the murders and his own suicide, the tape was aired on the national news. In the interview Smith claimed that he'd become a racist in direct reaction to the way in which he was, in his opinion, forced while in high school to accept white responsibility for the problems of minorities in the United States. This product of an excellent suburban school system where the teachers were actively engaged in an attempt to educate children to be free from racism, had taken away from his educational experience, exactly the opposite lesson (Ministry; NBC News).

That such a thing can happen sends a frightening message to all of us who are engaged in multicultural or anti-racism education and there have, of course, been

70

similar and equally powerful negative reactions to attempts to educate people on the evils of sexism, religious prejudice and prejudice against gays and lesbians as well. If a lesson can be learned from this it may be that explicitly didactic texts and lessons are more likely to elicit the kind of negative reaction that teachers and other people of good intent deplore. In my own teaching I've discovered over and over again that the majority of my students, regardless of their race, truly do resent any implication that they or theirs may in fact be responsible for racism, either directly or indirectly. In part this is an understandable reaction to the fact that the racist actions that appear in books, whether fictional or non-fictional, are indeed not their fault. Generally such events are depicted as happening in the past or simply somewhere else and most of my students are both unwilling and, in fact, incapable of seeing themselves as directly connected to the groups responsible for the problem. Indeed, on a gut level, most college students these days, perhaps most Americans, regardless of race or class, seem to see themselves as victims of prejudice. Whether the culprits are their elders, or the federal government, or minority groups, or the rich, they frequently see someone else as having been given preferential treatment by the powers that be. Many of my Caucasian male students, for example, despite all statistics to the contrary, are firmly convinced that when it comes to jobs and salary, they are unfairly disadvantaged in relationship to both minorities and women. That these beliefs are contrary to the truth, that they are being promulgated as a tactic for use in the subtle and virtually invisible class war that permeates much of American society, is something most young people cannot accept or even consider.

So, will less didactic books work better? There are increasing numbers of well-done, worthwhile picture books, like Sherry Garland's *The Lotus Seed* or *My Father's Boat*, for example, that accurately describe the plight of Vietnamese and other Southeast Asian families and their lives in the United States, but that do not explicitly go into the prejudice Southeast Asians find in this country. Are these stories, with their implicit message of tolerance more likely to be effective with children than a book like *Who Belongs Here?*, which goes head to head with racism? I don't pretend to have a final answer to this difficult question, though I suspect that, if one does exist, it lies somewhere in the middle. People who oppose change are often fond of saying that you can't legislate morality. On the other hand, we cannot afford to ignore racism, either. As Mark Twain suggested in his classic cautionary tale "The Man that Corrupted Hadleyburg" we cannot raise our children exclusively in a world of sweetness and light and hope that the very real evil in our world and in our nation will never touch them. To use a personal example, although we've done our best to protect our Korean-born daughter from racism here in western Wisconsin and, although to the best of my knowledge, she hasn't yet been scarred by it, she has run into it. As a happy two year old in a shopping cart she was once, with her mother standing not ten feet away, accosted by a group of teenagers who, paralleling Nary's experience in *Who Belongs Here?*, shouted at her "Look at that little gook baby, just sitting there. Somebody should kill all of them!" Virtually all of my daughter's Hmong-American and Korean-American friends report similar experiences. It's clear that, despite, perhaps because of, the Benjamin Smiths of the world, we have to continue to do our best. As teachers, as parents, as writers of books for and about children and their literature, we cannot ignore this battle.

Chapter Seven: Conclusion

"Multiculturalism" has become something of a dirty word in recent years, particularly in conservative intellectual and political circles. Attempts to explain minority cultures to the majority, to even claim some sort of continuing legitimacy for the cultures of immigrants once they've reached our shores, are often met with hostility and, what has become the ultimate put down, an insistence that the person arguing for multiculturalism is *merely* being "politically correct." It is clear, however, that those politicians and intellectuals who would deny the *fact* that the United States is already a multicultural nation are essentially living in a fantasy world. Well-to-do white, Anglo-Saxon males may still be able to insulate themselves and their families from the African, Hispanic, and Asian Americans who form the fastest growing segments of our population, but this can not help but change in the near future.

I live in Eau Claire, Wisconsin, just east of Minneapolis, Minnesota, which was one of the main re-settlement sites for the Hmong in the United States. Our region also has a significant Vietnamese population. I regularly have students from these ethnic groups in my children's literature classes at the University of Wisconsin-Stout, most of whom hope to become teachers. My eleven-year-old daughter (who, as I've already mentioned, is adopted Korean, which adds another interesting wrinkle to the situation) has several Hmong friends. Thus, I know from first-hand experience that Southeast Asians face serious problems in this country, some of them stemming from their own adjustment difficulties, some due to the prejudice and ignorance of others which they must deal with on an everyday basis. Many people are aware of the clashes between Vietnamese fishermen and the Ku Klux Klan in Texas over the years, but a lot of other problems rarely make the national news. Vietnamese youth gangs are becoming a regular part of the urban scene in Texas and Los Angeles, while Hmong youth gangs are a problem in Los Angeles, Minneapolis and, increasingly, in small midwestern cities such as Eau Claire. Thousands of older Hmong, most of whom were forced to flee their homeland because they collaborated with American troops during the secret war in Laos, have never been able to acclimatize to life in the U.S and, despite what President Clinton has been saying in recent months, are still in danger of losing much of their welfare and medical support. The stress caused by this threat has already led to an increase in domestic abuse, suicide, and family-related murders in the Hmong population. Busing and segregation have once again become hot issues in several southwestern and midwestern cities because of rapidly increasing Southeast Asian populations. A year or so ago the Superintendent of the Wausau, Wisconsin public schools lost her job over her support for busing to racially balance the schools.

Unfortunately, few of the picture books that I've mentioned in this volume deal very effectively with these specific issues. As I've shown there's quite a bit about the horrors of war, relocation, and post-traumatic stress disorder, the problems Southeast Asians brought with them from the old country. There's relatively little on the level of picture books, however, about the new problems that have grown up in the United States, particularly racism and gangs. It may be too much to expect of any one book, particularly a picture book, that it should cover all aspects of an issue. I was somewhat surprised to discover, however, that Sherry Garland's recent and otherwise excellent *My Father's Boat*, the first picture book to deal with Vietnamese-American fishermen, didn't even mention the racial violence that has haunted the Texas Gulf Coast over the past two decades. In contrast, Margy Burns Knight's *Who Belongs Here?*, although a bit overly didactic perhaps, stands out as the most clearsighted and honest attempt to handle racism in practical terms on a child's level. Surat's *Angel Child, Dragon Child*, though its heart is in the right place and it is certainly a good book to start with, does little more than preach the unfortunately simplistic message that communication and understanding will solve most problems, a message that too often does not prove to be the case.

Although a small number of YA novels also address these issues, the only other books that I've found that even mention racism and Southeast Asian-American gangs and that may be accessible to younger children are two chapter books, Sara Gogol's *A Mien Family* and Stephanie St. Pierre's *Teenage Refugees from Cambodia Speak Out*. Gogol's well-done work of non-fiction about the Mien, a group of people closely related to the Hmong, specifically addresses the concerns of the older generation of immigrants that their children, in breaking away from the old customs, are increasingly becoming involved in criminal activity. As Ta Jow Saechao, a Mien father of seven suggests "Children need to learn American values in order to succeed in this country" (49), but he and his wife are concerned with the way some of their friends have lost control of their children. Ta Jow has kept his family in Portland, Oregon, rather than joining relatives in California in large part because of the gang activity in Los Angeles. This is apparently a common complaint among older Hmong as well who feel "that they are unable to discipline their children under American law and that [this], coupled with the lack of respect afforded elders, increasingly propels teens into gang violence" (*Hmong in America*, 77). In St. Pierre's book, which largely consists of a series of interviews with Cambodian teenagers, a young man named Tithra explains that "gangs are mostly a way for us to be with other people who can understand, who have the same kind of background....[it's] a way to feel that I wasn't so different from other kids in school" (25-26). A new and worthwhile treatment of Hmong gangs, although it isn't aimed at children, can be found in Lillian Faderman and Ghia Xiong's *I Begin My Life All Over* (1998).

Of course, as already mentioned, novels and works of non-fiction aimed at Young Adults cover some of these issues in more detail and Jan Susina's well-done but now somewhat dated article "'Tell him about Vietnam': Vietnamese-Americans in Contemporary American Children's Literature" offers a solid introduction to such books. In the beginning picture book *Onion Tears* by Diana Kidd, for example, Nam-Huong, a Vietnamese refugee child living with a foster mother because her parents are lost and presumed dead, is teased by the Australian children of European origin, who make fun of her name, her odd lunches, and her eccentric bicycle, but for the most part they're simply responding to her unwillingness to become one of the group. When she opens up to them, they accept her immediately. The early and quite graphic *A Long Way from Home* (1980) by Maureen Wartski and Jamie Gilson's *Hello, My Name is Scrambled Eggs* (1985) deal with racism on a more serious level, but, again, were written for older children. Another novel, Sherry Garland's *Song of the Buffalo Boy (1992)*, concerns racist attitudes towards the Amerasian children left behind in Vietnam after the war. To this day, however, few books, even on the YA level, deal with Southeast Asian gangs (one notable exception being Sherry Garland's *Shadow of the Dragon*), nor are there any YA novels dealing with the Hmong or Mien experience in America at all

I suggested earlier that few of the picture books under discussion devote much space, or indeed, any space at all to an examination of who was responsible for the various wars that did so much damage to Vietnam, Laos, and Cambodia. Although it is impossible to read the authors' minds, of course, or make any kind of definitive judgment as to why this is the case, it may be worthwhile to present a few possibilities. As has already been suggested, most of the books are told from a child's viewpoint and thus cannot realistically be expected to contain much in the way of an ideological perspective. Further, since the books under consideration are aimed primarily at children ages six through ten, it could well be argued that the authors might consider any attempt to assign blame or give complex reasons for the fighting to be inappropriate. To the extent that the characters in the books, both real and fictional, do demonstrate an ideological perspective, however, it seems to consist primarily of a simple, straightforward love of the land and its people, with no real

76

interest in the politics emanating from Saigon, Hanoi, Phnom Penh, Vientiane, or, for that matter, Washington, D.C. For most of the characters in these books, both fictional and non-fictional, war seems to have been simply a dirty business that one had to deal with for purely practical reasons. Patriotism, in the flag waving sense, doesn't appear to have been particularly relevant. If someone attacked you, you either ran away or fought back. For example, although we are often told that many Hmong fought bravely on the United States's side during the secret war in Laos, which is true, it is rarely mentioned, as Dia Cha makes clear in *Dia's Story Cloth* and as discussed in *Hmong in America* (29) a book not intended for children, that other Hmong fought on the side of the Communist Pathet Lao. Nor is it widely mentioned that many of the Hmong who fought on the United States side were essentially conscripts. In *Hmong in America* we are told that "Villagers came under intense pressure from both sides to join their cause. Local neutrality, like national neutrality became difficult to maintain....Boys as young as 10 were drafted to fight" (45-47). In *A Mien Family* Ta Jow Saechao, a decorated veteran of the U.S.-supported army that fought the Pathet Lao, reveals that originally "He had no choice about becoming a soldier. `If I refused, I would be arrested'" (24). In Minfong Ho's fine YA novel *The Clay Marble* we are introduced to a sort of patriotism, in the form of young Cambodian military men, some of them Khmer Rouge, some the supposedly anti-Communist Khmer Serei, who spout phrases like "As part of the great revolutionary cause...we must wage a struggle against the puppets and lackeys of our enemies. We must strive to be anti-colonialist, anti-Vietnamese, anti-imperialist..." (141), but Ho makes it clear that such language has little meaning to the refugees to whom it is addressed. The young men who join the army do so either because it will provide their homeless families with food and relative safety, or because they've been caught up in the perverse excitement of military parades and guns that has always attracted the young and foolish to war.

Can anything else be determined about the ideological stances of the various books? Two of the picture books, as has been noted, do *implicitly* tag the United States as an aggressor--*The Little Weaver of Thai-Yen Village* and *Sweet Dried*

Apples--both have protagonists who suffer under aerial bombardments of a sort only the United States was capable of carrying out. Most of the other fiction, however, makes no real attempt to lay the blame at anyone's door. The non-fiction accounts also tend either to strive for ideological neutrality or, alternately, to give the standard pro-American interpretation of the war, that is that the United States intervened at the request of the legitimate government of South Vietnam, did its best for all concerned, and then got out. To some extent this may be an issue about which the authors have very little choice; the odds of a children's book being published in the United States that says negative things about the relatively recent actions of the U.S. government are rather small, at least where the major presses are concerned. Controversy is generally not something with which our increasingly corporate publishing industry is particularly comfortable. It has only been in the past decade or so, after all, that children's books have appeared which have had the temerity to criticize the United States government's policy concerning Native Americans in the nineteenth century, or for that matter Columbus' policies towards Indians in the fifteenth and sixteenth centuries. Sometimes, however, the careful reader will find pro-American distortions in fact, or at least interpretation, in these books. For example in Muriel Stanek's *We Came from Vietnam*, we are told that "Finally, an agreement was signed to stop the fighting between the two Vietnams. The United States forces left. But soon North Vietnam brought in more troops. Saigon, the capital city of South Vietnam, fell into Communist hands in 1975." Stanek's account certainly makes it sound as if there were no longer any Americans involved in the war at the time of the fall of Saigon, which, of course, was hardly the case. In her controversial 1979 study *America Revised, History Schoolbooks in the Twentieth Century*, a work which remains as relevant today as when it was first published, the noted historian Frances FitzGerald excoriates American history books for children for their wild inaccuracies and gross, politically-motivated misinterpretations of the historical record. Parodying the sometimes inane way in which such texts attempted to explain the war in Southeast Asia, FitzGerald writes, "the war kept on growing until it became `full-fledged'; many

Americans were `deeply troubled' by it; and yet, in spite of temporary halts in the bombing of North Vietnam, in spite of appeals to the North Vietnamese leaders, and in spite of negotiations and troop withdrawals, the war kept on going--until it finally stopped" (126). She labels this "the crabgrass theory of the Vietnam War because, like crabgrass, the war just happened. This phrase neatly summarizes the ideological content of most of the books being considered in this study. In this context, the attempt to avoid any and all controversy, it may also be worth noting the complete lack of mention, at least within the context of picture books, of the heavy involvement of the Hmong in the Opium trade, despite the fact that it was widely grown and used by Laotian Hmong males in the time just prior to the war (Ovesen, 12).

For the most part, the authors of the picture and beginning chapter books I have discussed here do not appear to be particularly interested in teaching children about the complex political ideologies behind the various wars in Southeast Asia and perhaps this is for the best. Rather, most of them clearly see their primary purpose as being to give a positive portrayal of the common people of Vietnam, Laos, and Cambodia, both at home and in the United States. They show us children, women, and men who went through hell during the wars and as refugees, but who have come to the United States over the past 25 years and worked hard to make a place for themselves. These people want to be Americans, but at the same time the ties to the old countries remain strong, and well they should. Ultimately, it is all about roots, about family, about having a history of cultural achievement. Refugees, coming to this country with nothing, can stand as proud as the next person as long as they know that their people, their culture, is valuable. Southeast Asian children growing up in the United States must have available to them books and other media, for example the Hmong *pa'ndau*, which tell them who they are, where they came from, and why it matters. Only by having respect for their own backgrounds can these children overcome the scars left by war and camp life, and gain the self-respect necessary to become successful and happy adults.

Ultimately, then, books like Dia's *Story Cloth, Dara's Cambodian New Year,*

The Whispering Cloth, *The Gift*, *Who Belongs Here?*, *Sweet Dried Apples*, *The Lotus Seed* and *Angel Child, Dragon Child*, are important and should be made widely available for two reasons. First, because they can help American children of Southeast Asian background hold on to and recognize the value of their heritage. Secondly, and equally important, because they can also help children of other ethnicities understand and respect what is, after all, merely the latest in the long line of important immigrant groups who have made America what it is today.

Bibliography

Picture Books

Breckler, Rosemary. *Hoang Breaks the Lucky Teapot*. Illustrated by Adrian Frankel. Boston: Houghton Mifflin, 1992.

_____. *Sweet Dried Apples*, illustrated by Deborah Kogan Ray. Boston: Houghton Mifflin, 1996.

Cha, Dia. *Dia's Story Cloth*, illustrated by Cue and Nhia Thao Cha. New York: Lee & Low, 1996.

Chiemruom, Sothea. *Dara's Cambodian New Year*, illustrated by Dam Nang Pin. Simon & Schuster, 1994.

Garland, Sherry. *The Lotus Seed*, illustrated by Tatsuro Kiuchi. San Diego: Harcourt, Brace, 1993.

_____. *My Father's Boat*, illustrated by Ted Rand. New York: Scholastic, 1998.

Jeffers, Susan. *Brother Eagle, Sister Sky: A Message from Chief Seattle*. New York: Dial, 1993.

Knight, Margy Burns. *Who Belongs Here?*, illustrated by Anne Sibley O'Brien. Gardiner, MN: Tilbury, 1993.

Lee, Jeanne M. *Silent Lotus*. New York: Farrar, Straus and Giroux, 1991.

Marchant, Brian and Heather Marchant. *A Boy Named Chong*, illustrated by Ya Lee. Green Bay, WI: Project Chong, 1992.

_____. *The World Without "F," Chong Learns the Alphabet*, illustrated by Ya Lee. Green Bay, WI: Project Chong, 1996.

McKay, Jr., Lawrence. *Journey Home*, illustrated by Dom & Keunhee Lee. New York: Lee & Low, 1998.

Shea, Pegi Deitz. *The Whispering Cloth*, illustrated by Anita Riggio and You Yang. Honesdale, PN: Boyds Mill, 1995.

Surat, Michele Maria. *Angel Child, Dragon Child*, illustrated by Vo-Dinh Mai. New York: Scholastic, 1983, rpt. 1989.

Trân Khánh Tuyêt *The Little Weaver of Thai-Yen Village*, translated by Christopher N.H. Jenkins and the author, illustrated by Nancy Hom. San Francisco: Children's Book Press, 1977, rev. 1987.

Tran Kim-Lan. *Têt: The New Year*, illustrated by Mai Vo-Dinh. New York: Simon & Schuster, 1992.

Xiong, Ia. *The Gift, The Hmong New Year*, illustrated by Gou Run-Lin. Los Angeles: Pacific Asia Press, 1996.

Yolen, Jane. *Encounter*, illustrated by David Shannon. New York: Harcourt Brace, 1992.

Folktales

Beard, Tim, and others, eds. *In the Old, Old Days (Loz-Hnoi, Loz-Hnoi Uov).* Berkeley, CA. Laotian Handcraft Project, 1993. , Volume 1 in the Traditional Stories of the Iu-Mienh.

Brown, Marcia. *Cinderella, or The Little Glass Slipper.* New York: Scribners, 1954.

Child, Frances James, ed. *The English and Scottish Popular Ballads*, Vol. I, (1882). New York: Dover, 1965.

Coburn, Jewell Reinhart. *Angkat, The Cambodian Cinderella*, illustrated by Eddie Flotte. Arcadia, CA: Shen's Books, 1998.

_____ and Duong Van Quyen. *Beyond the East Wind*, illustrated by Nena Grigovian Ullberg. Thousand Oaks, CA: Burn, Hart, 1976.

_____ with Tzexa Cherta Lee. *Jouanah, A Hmong Cinderella*, illustrated by Anne Sibley O'Brien. Arcadia, CA: Shen's Books, 1996.

_____.*Ntsuag Nos, Ib Tug Cinderella Hmoob*, illustrated by Anne Sibley O'Brien. Arcadia, CA: Shen's Books, 1996 (Hmong language version of *Jouanah*).

Garland, Sherry. *Why Ducks Sleep on One Leg*, illustrated by Jean and Mou-sien Tseng. New York: Scholastic, 1993.

Giacchino-Baker, Rosalie, ed. *Stories from Laos: Folktales and Cultures of the Lao, Hmong, Khammu, and Iu-Mien.* Los Angeles: Pacific Asia, 1995.

_____. *The Story of Mah, A Hmong "Romeo and Juliet" Folktale*, illustrated by Lillian Shao. Los Angeles: Pacific Asia Press, 1997

Grimm, Jacob, and Wilhelm Grimm. *The Complete Grimm's Fairy Tales*, with an introduction by Padraic Colum, illustrated by Josef Scharl. New York: Pantheon, 1944.

Ho, Minfong. *The Two Brothers*, illustrated by Jean & Mou-Sien Tseng. New York: Lothrop, Lee & Shepard, 1995.

_____ and Saphan Ros. *Brother Rabbit, A Cambodian Tale*, illustrated by Jennifer Hewitson. New York: Lothrop, Lee & Shepard, 1997.

Johnson, Charles, and Ava Dale Johnson, eds. *Six Hmong Folk Tales Retold in English*, illustrated by Xiong Lia Vang. St. Paul, MN: Macalister College Lingquistics Department, 1981.

_____ and Se Yang, eds. *Dab Neeg Hmoob: Myths, Legends and Folk Tales from the Hmong of Laos*, Second Edition. St. Paul, MN: Linquistics Department, Macalester College, 1985, 1992.

Kha, Dang Manh, and Ann Nolan Clark. *In the Land of Small Dragon: A Vietnamese*

Folktale, illustrated by Tony Chen. New York: Viking, 1979.

Lee, Jeanne M. *Toad Is the Uncle of Heaven*. New York: Henry Holt, 1985.

Lewis, Beverly. *Cows in the House*, illustrated by Chi Chung. Minneapolis: Bethany House, 1998.

Livo, Norma J., and Dia Cha. *Folk Stories of the Hmong Peoples of Laos, Thailand and Vietnam*. Englewood, CO: Libraries Unlimited, 1991.

Louie, Ai-Ling. *Yeh-Shen A Cinderella Story from China,* illustrated by Ed Young. New York: Philomel, 1982.

Lucas, Alice. *How the Farmer Tricked the Evil Demon,* illustrated by Kosal Kong, translated by Ia Xiong. Los Angeles: Pacific Asia Press, 1994.

Lum, Darrel. *The Golden Slipper*, illustrated by Makiko Nagano. Nc: Troll, 1994.

Neak, Touch. *The Mountain of the Men & the Mountain of the Women*, retold by Alice Lucas. San Francisco: Voices of Liberty, 1990.

Nielsen, Kay. *The Wishing Pearl and Other Tales of Vietnam*, trans by Lam Chan Quan. Irving-on-Hudson, NY: Harvey House, 1969.

Numrich, Charles H. *Living Tapestries, Folk Tales of the Hmong.* Lima, OH: Fairway Press, 1985.

Perrault, Charles. *Complete Fairy Tales*, translated by A. E. Johnson, illustrated by W. Heath Robinson. New York: Dodd, Mead, 1961.

Sayavong, James, ed. *Asian Folktales Retold by Asian Bilingual Students from Room #17*. Milwaukee: Milwaukee Public Schools, 1991.

Shepard, Aaron. *The Crystal Heart, A Vietnamese Legend*, illustrated by Joseph Daniel Fiedler. New York: Atheneum, 1998.

Spagnoli, Cathy. *Asian Tales and Tellers*. Little Rock, Arkansas: August House, 1998.

_____. *Judge Rabbit Helps the Fish*, illustrated by Kat Thacker. Bothel, WA: The Wright Group, 1995.

_____. *Thao Kham, the Pebble Shooter*, illustrated by Chi Chung. Bothel, WA: The Wright Group, 1995.

Thao, Cher. *Only a Toad*, adapted by Brian & Heather Marchant, illustrated by Ya Lee. Green Bay, WI: Project Chong, 1993.

Tran Van Dien. *Once in Vietnam (Ngay Xua O Que Huong Toi)*, illustrated by Kim Bang. Lincolnwood, IL: National Textbook, 1994.

Vathanaprida, Supaporn. *Thai Tales, Folktales of Thailand*, ed. by Margaret Read MacDonald, illustrated by Boonsong Rohitasuke. Englewood, CO: Libraries Unlimited, 1994.

Vang, Lue, and Judy Lewis. *Grandmother's Path, Grandfather's Way*.Rancho Cordova, CA: Vang and Lewis, 1990.

Vuong, Lynette Dyer. *The Brocaded Slipper and Other Vietnamese Tales*, illustrated by Vo-Dinh Mai. (1982). New York: Harper Trophy, 1992.

_____. *The Golden Carp and Other Tales from Vietnam*, illustrated by Manabu Saito. New York: Lothrop, Lee & Shepard, 1993.

Wall, Lina Mao. *Judge Rabbit and the Tree Spirit, A Foktale from Cambodia,* adapted by Cathy Spagnoli, illustrated by Nancy Hom. San Francisco:

Children's Book Press, 1991.

Xiong, Blia. *Nine-in-One, Grr! Grr!*, adapted by Cathy Spagnoli, illustrated by Nancy Hom. San Francisco: Children's Book Press, 1989.

Yang, May, Phoua Thao, and Se Yang. *Yer and the Tiger,* edited by Ava-Dale Johnson, illustrated by Danny Rodriquez. St. Paul: Free People Publications, 1981.

Non-Fiction for Children

Blanc, Felice. *I Am Vietnamese American.* New York: Rosen/PowerKids Press. Part of the *Our American Family* series.

Brittan, Dolly. *The Hmong.* New York: Rosen/PowerKids Press, 1997. Part of the *Celebrating the People and Civilizations of Southeast Asia* series.

_____. *The People of Cambodia.* New York: Rosen/PowerKids Press, 1998

_____. *The People of Laos.* New York: Rosen/PowerKids Press, 1998

_____. *The People of Vietnam.* New York: Rosen/PowerKids Press, 1998.

Ganeri, Anita. *Southeast Asia.* New York: Franklin Watts, 1995. Part of the *Places and People* series.

Garland, Sherry. *Vietnam, Rebuilding a Nation.* Minneapolis: Dillon, 1990. Part of the *Discovering Our Heritage* series.

Gogol, Sara. *A Mien Family.* Minneapolis: Lerner, 1996. Part of the *Journey Between Two Worlds* series.

Goldfarb, Mace. *Fighters, Refugees, Immigrants,* photographs by the author. Minneapolis: Carolrhoda Books, 1982.

Graff, Nancy Price. *Where the River Runs,* photographs by Richard Howard. New York: Scholastic, 1993.

Hoyt-Goldsmith, Diane. *Hoang Anh, A Vietnamese-American Boy,* photographs by Lawrence Midgale. New York: Holiday House, 1992.

Huynh Quang Nhuong. *The Land I Lost: Adventures of a Boy in Vietnam.* New York: Harper & Row, 1982.

_____. *Water Buffalo Days,* illustrated by Jean and Mou-sien Tseng. New York: HarperCollins, 1997.

Jacobsen, Karen. *Laos.* Chicago: Childrens Press, 1991. Part of the *New True Book* series.

Kalman, Bobbie. *Vietnam: The Culture.* New York: Crabtree, 1996. Part of The Lands, Peoples, and Cultures series.

_____. *Vietnam: The Land.* New York: Crabtree, 1996.

_____. *Vietnam: The People.* New York: Crabtree, 1996.

Kilborne, Sarah S. *Leaving Vietnam, The True Story of Tuan Ngo,* illustrated by Melissa Sweet. New York: Simon & Schuster, 1999.

Lorbiecki, Marybeth. *Children of Vietnam,* photographs by Paul P. Rome. Minneapolis: Carolrhoda Books, 1997. Part of *The World's Children* series.

MacMillan, Dianne and Dorothy Freeman. *My Best Friend, Duc Tran: Meeting a Vietnamese-American Family.* New York: Simon & Schuster, 1987. Part of the *My Best Friend* series.

McKay, Susan. *Vietnam*. Milwaukee: Gareth Stevens Publishing, 1997. Part of the *Festivals of the World* series.

Murphy, Nora. *A Hmong Family*. Minneapolis: Lerner, 1997. Part of the *Journey Between Two Worlds* series.

O'Connor, Karen. *Dan Thuy's New Life in America*, photographs by the author. Minneapolis: Lerner, 1992.

Rutledge, Paul. *The Vietnamese in America*. Minneapolis: Lerner, 1987.

Schmidt, Jeremy and Ted Wood. *Two Lands, One Heart. An American Boy's Journey to His Mother's Vietnam*. New York: Walker, 1995.

Smith, Linda. *Dat's New Year*. London: A&C Black, 1999.

St. Pierre, Stephanie. *Teenage Refugees from Cambodia Speak Out*. New York: Rosen, 1995. Part of the *In Their Own Voices* series.

Stanek, Muriel. *We Came from Vietnam*, photography by Wm. Franklin McMahon. Morton Grove, IL: Albert Whitman, 1985.

Tooze, Ruth. *Our Rice Village in Cambodia*, illustrated by Ezra Jack Keats. New York: Viking, 1963.

Children's Chapter Books and Young Adult Novels

Baillie, Allan. *Little Brother* (1985). New York: Puffin, 1992.

Bennett, Jack. *The Voyage of the Lucky Dragon*. New York: Prentice-Hall, 1981.

Clark, Ann Nolan. *To Stand Against the Wind*. New York: Viking, 1978.

Crew, Linda. *Children of the River*. New York: Delacorte, 1989.

Garland, Sherry. *Shadow of the Dragon*. New York: Harcourt, Brace, 1993
_____. *Song of the Buffalo Boy*. New York: Harcourt, Brace, 1992

Gilson, Jamie. *Hello, My Name is Scrambled Eggs*, illustrated by John Wallner. New York: Lothrop, Lee & Shepard, 1985.

Glass, Tom. *Even A Little is Something. Stories of Nong*, illustrated by Elena Gerard. North Haven, CN: Linnet, 1997.

Graham, Gail. *Crossfire: A Vietnam Novel*, illus. by David Stone Martin. New York: Pantheon, 1972.

Ho, Minfong. *The Clay Marble*. New York: Farrar, Straus, Giroux, 1991.

Holmes, Mary Z. *Dust of Life,* illustrated by Geri Strigenz. Austin, TX: Raintree, 1992.

Kidd, Diana. *Onion Tears,* illustrated by Lucy Montgomery (1989). New York: Orchard, 1991.

Paterson, Katherine. *Park's Quest*. New York: Penguin, 1988.

Pevsner, Stella, and Fay Tang. *Sing for Your Father, Su Phan*. New York: Clarion, 1997.

Staples, Suzanne Fisher. *Shabanu: Daughter of the Wind*. NY: Knopf, 1989.

Wartski, Maureen Crane. *A Boat to Nowhere*. Philadelphia: Westminster, 1980.
_____. *A Long Way from Home*. Philadelphia: Westminster, 1980.

Whelan, Gloria *Goodbye, Vietnam*. New York: Random House, 1992.

Secondary Sources: Articles and Shorter Works

Baillie, Allan. "Pol Pot's Reign of Terror: Why Write About It for Children?" in *Battling Dragons: Issues and Controversy in Children's Literature*, ed. by Susan Lehr. Portsmouth, NH: Heinemann, 1995, pp 148-154.

Eau Claire Leader Telegram, July 26, 1999: 4A.

Ho, Minfong. "The Shaping of *The Clay Marble*" in *Battling Dragons: Issues and Controversy in Children's Literature*, ed. by Susan Lehr. Portsmouth, NH: Heinemann, 1995, pp 141-147.

Jameson, R. D. "Cinderella in China (1932), rpt. In *Cinderella, A Folklore Casebook*, ed. Alan Dundes. New York: Garland, 1982: 71-97.

Lindow, Sandra J. "Trauma and Recovery in Ursula K. LeGuin's *Wonderful Alexander*: Animal as Guide Through the Inner Space of the Unconscious." In *Foundation: The International Journal of Science Fiction* (Summer 1997): 32-38.

Liu, Li. "Hoang Breaks the Lucky Teapot" in *The New Press Guide to Multicultural Resources for Young Readers,* edited by Daphne Muse. New York: The New Press, 1997, p. 412.

Ministry in the Midst of Hate and Violence—"Fourth of July Weekend Shootings": gbgm-umc.org/programs/antihate/index.html, accessed August 1, 1999. Information gathered from various articles found on this website, sponsored by the United Methodist Church, which collects newspaper articles on racism from around the country.

Muse, Daphne. "Dia's Story Cloth: The Hmong People's Journey of Freedom" in *The New Press Guide to Multicultural Resources for Young Readers,* edited by Daphne Muse. New York: The New Press, 1997, p. 453.

NBC News story, broadcast July 7, 1999.

Rhodes, Lisa. "Onion Tears" in in *The New Press Guide to Multicultural Resources for Young Readers,* edited by Daphne Muse. New York: The New Press, 1997, pp. 455-56.

Susina, Jan. "'Tell him about Vietnam': Vietnamese-Americans in Contemporary American Children's Literature," *Children's Literature Association Quarterly*, Vol. 16 (Summer 1991): 58-63.

Zuwiya, Nancy. "Death and Life in the Literature of Southeast Asia," *SIGNAL*, Vol. 19 (Spring/Summer 1995): 39-43.

Secondary Sources: Books

Beilke, Patricia F., and Frank J. Sciara. *Selected Materials for and about Hispanic and East Asian Children and Young People*. Hamden, CN: Library Professional, 1986.

Bordewich, Fergus M. *Killing the White Man's Indian: Reinventing Native Americans at the End of the Twentieth Century*. New York: Doubleday, 1996.

Brunvand, Jan Harold. *The Study of American Folklore.* 4th ed. New York: Norton, 1998.

Chang, Kou, and Sheila Pinkel. *Kou Chang's Story: The Journey of a Laotian Hmong Refugee Family.* Rochester, NY: Visual Studies Workshop Press, 1993.

Chen, Lai Nam. *Images of Southeast Asia in Children's Books.* Singapore: Singapore University Press, 1981.

Criddle, JoAn D. *Bamboo and Butterflies: From Refugee to Citizen.* Second edition. Dixon, CA: East West Bridge, 1992.

_____ andTeeda Butt Mam. *To Destroy You Is No Loss: The Odyssey of a Cambodian Family.* Updated edition. Dixon, CA: East West Bridge, 1995.

Faderman, Lillian, with Ghia Xiong. *I Begin My Life All Over: The Hmong and the American Immigrant Experience.* Boston: Beacon, 1998.

Fadiman, Anne. *The Spirit Catches You and You Fall Down: A Hmong Child, Her American Doctors, and the Collison of Two Cultures.* New York: Farrar, Straus and Giroux, 1997.

FitzGerald, Frances. *America Revised, History Schoolbooks in the Twentieth Century.* Boston: Little Brown, 1979.

Giacchino-Baker, Rosalie, with Tina Bacon and Kathy Felts. *Teacher's Resource Book for The Story of Mah.* Los Angeles: Pacific Asia Press, 1997.

Hein, Jeremy. *From Vietnam, Laos, and Cambodia: A Refugee Experience in the United States.* New York: Twayne, 1995.

Herman, Judith Lewis. *Trauma and Recovery.* New York: Basic Books, 1992.

Jenkins, Esther C., and Mary C. Austin. *Literature for Children About Asians and Asian Americans Analysis and Annotated Bibliography, With Additional Readings for Adults.* New York: Greenwood Press, 1987. *Bibliographies and Indexes in World Literature*, Number 12.

Knight, Margy Burns, and Thomas V. Chan. *Who Belongs Here? Activity Guide,* illustrated by Anne Sibley O'Brien. Gardiner, MN: Tilbury, 1994.

Moore, David L. *Dark Sky, Dark Land. Stories of the Hmong Boy Scouts of Troop 100.* Eden Prairie, MN: Tseera, 1989.

Muse, Daphne, editor. *The New Press Guide to Multicultural Resources for Young Readers.* New York: The New Press, 1997.

Ovesen, Jan. *A Minority Enters the Nation State: A Case Study of a Hmong Community in Vientiane Province, Laos.* Uppsala Research Reports in Cultural Anthropology, No. 14. Uppsala, Sweden: Uppsala University, 1995.

Pfaff, Tim. *Hmong in America; Journey from a Secret War.* Eau Claire, WI: Chippewa Valley Museum Press, 1995.

Rolland, Barbara J., and Houa Vue Moua. *Trail Through the Mists.* Eau Claire, WI: Eagles Printing, 1994.

Takaki, Ronald. *Strangers from a Different Shore: A History of Asian Americans.* New York: Penguin, 1989.

Tenhula, John. *Voices from Southeast Asia: The Refugee Experience in the United States.* New York: Holmes and Meier, 1991.

Terr, Lenore *Too Scared to Cry: How Trauma Affects Children and Ultimately Us All*. New York: Harper & Row, 1990.

Ting, Nai-Tung. *The Cinderella Cycle in China and Indo-China*. Helsinki: Suomalainen Tiedeakatemia, 1974.

Warner, Marina. *From the Beast to the Blond, On Fairy Tales and Their Tellers*. New York: Farrar, Straus and Giroux, 1994.

Wills, Garry. *John Wayne's America: The Politics of Celebrity*. New York: Simon & Schuster, 1997.

Index

STUDIES IN AMERICAN LITERATURE